高职高专会展专业新形态教材

会展英语听说教程

（第2版）

陈　颖　李世平 主编

吴殿龙　张　威　于海波 副主编

清华大学出版社

北京

内容简介

本书以全新的视角实践了"会展与英语一体化、理论与实践一体化"的教学理念,充分体现了高职高专会展英语"以实践为核心、以英语为主线、以会展为背景"的教学模式,重点培养学生的英语听说交际能力。

本书包括会议和展览两大部分,每部分由 8 个单元组成,共计 16 个单元。内容包括会议准备、会议选址、会议预订、会议接待与登记、会议室布置及会议设施、开幕式和闭幕式、会议餐饮服务、会后观光、展会特性确认、贸易展、展会策划、展会营销与推广、展会邀请、展品介绍、展品物流与运输、展会风险管理等,涵盖会展服务与管理的主要内容。每个单元内容包括背景知识、热身活动、示范对话、实用句型、实践实训项目等。

本书不仅可以作为高职高专院校会展专业的教材,还可以作为旅游、酒店、商务英语等专业学生的教材、参考书,以及有志于从事会展工作的专业人士、管理人员、翻译人员的参考资料。

为便于教师教学以及学生学习和参考,本书配有系统的教学大纲、习题库、音频资料、参考译文、术语表以及课件等教辅材料。读者可扫描书中二维码以获取音频资料,还可以扫描封底二维码以获取其余配套资源。

图书在版编目(CIP)数据

会展英语听说教程 / 陈颖, 李世平主编. -- 2版.
北京 : 清华大学出版社, 2025. 2. -- (高职高专会展专业新形态教材). -- ISBN 978-7-302-68128-1

Ⅰ. G245
中国国家版本馆CIP数据核字第2025EE3147号

责任编辑:刘远菁
封面设计:常雪影
版式设计:方加青
责任校对:成凤进
责任印制:刘 菲

出版发行:清华大学出版社
   网 址:https://www.tup.com.cn,https://www.wqxuetang.com
   地 址:北京清华大学学研大厦 A 座   邮 编:100084
   社 总 机:010-83470000   邮 购:010-62786544
   投稿与读者服务:010-62776969,c-service@tup.tsinghua.edu.cn
   质 量 反 馈:010-62772015,zhiliang@tup.tsinghua.edu.cn
印 装 者:三河市天利华印刷装订有限公司
经 销:全国新华书店
开 本:185mm×260mm   印 张:12.5   字 数:251 千字
版 次:2016 年 6 月第 1 版 2025 年 2 月第 2 版 印 次:2025 年 2 月第 1 次印刷
定 价:49.80 元

产品编号:108667-01

前　言

近年来，随着我国社会主义经济高质量发展，会展业发展迅猛，在经济社会发展中的作用日益凸显，成为现代服务业新的增长点，享有城市经济的"晴雨表"和"助推器"等美誉。

由于中国会展业的蓬勃发展，国际化、专业化步伐的加快，对会展专业人才的需求也越来越旺盛，对从业人员的要求也越来越高。现代会展业发展需要的是"既能熟练进行会展行业的规范操作与管理，又能熟练运用英语进行交流与沟通"的复合型会展人才。这是行业发展趋势对专业会展人才素质的必然要求，也是高职会展英语教学应该肩负的使命和需要实现的目标。本教材就是在综合考虑行业实际需要和现有教学资源的基础上编写的。

本再版书在第1版的基础上进行了全面的更新与完善。书中对话的背景信息(如展会届次及年份、展会名称信息等)已更新，在会议及展会设备、设施等方面，坚持与时俱进，紧跟当代科技和新业态发展的步伐，摒弃传真、幻灯机、投影仪等过时的设备，取而代之的是网络及新型数字化平台及模拟仿真设备等，同时将线上展会这种新型展会形式增加进来。

本书的特色

1. 职业特色鲜明，专业特色突出。本教材涵盖会展业服务和管理的主要内容，将职业技能的训练贯穿于英语学习中，使学习者感到明确的职业指向性。

2. 专业性和实用性强。在示范对话模块中，设置具体的对话情景，并在内容上与会展活动实践对接，帮助学生通过示范对话内容的学习和训练，掌握英语会话技巧和会展工作相关技能。

3. 注重能力训练。每个单元结尾都科学设计、精心组织综合训练内容，注重英语听说能力的培养和职业素质的养成。

4. 使用对象广泛。本教材不仅可以作为高职高专院校会展专业的教材，还可以作为旅游、酒店、商务英语等专业学生的教材、参考书，以及有志于从事会展工作的专业人士、管理人员、翻译人员的参考资料。

5. 为便于教师教学以及学生学习和参考，本书配有系统的教学大纲、习题库、音频资料、参考译文、术语表以及课件等教辅材料。读者可扫描书中二维码以获取音频资料，还可以扫描封底二维码以获取其余配套资源。

　　本书由长春职业技术学院会展英语主讲教师陈颖和旅澳学者李世平教授主编，陈颖老师负责定稿、文本翻译，以及编写第5～10单元，李世平老师负责统稿和编写第1～4单元。其他参编人员具体分工：张威老师编写第11～12单元；吴殿龙老师编写第13～14单元；于海波老师编写第15～16单元。

　　美籍教师Victor Maneilley和Annie Gardiner担任本书主审并负责主要的录音工作。美籍教师Douglas Humphreys和科特迪瓦籍教师Beuger Marie Michelle Nancy负责第2版教材部分对话的录音工作。

　　本书在编写过程中得到了众多同行和相关人士的大力支持，清华大学出版社的编辑对本书的结构安排以及内容选取等方面提出了许多宝贵建议，在此一并致谢。

　　由于编者经验和水平有限，书中难免存在不当之处，敬请广大专家及读者不吝指正。反馈邮箱：wkservice@vip.163.com。

编者

2024年8月

目 录

Part One
会议英语 English for Conventions

Part Two
展览英语 English for Exhibitions

Part
One

会议英语
English for Conventions

Unit One

会议准备
Preparing for the Meeting

Teaching Targets 教学目标

- To learn how to prepare for a meeting
- To master some basic guiding principles for preparing a meeting
- To grasp some useful words, phrases, and key sentences related to the topic
- To hold conversations concerning this topic

背景知识
Background Knowledge

为保证会议的成功，会前必须做好充分的准备。会议顺利与否，关键在于会前是否做了精心策划。会议的准备工作一般包括会议的发起、会议召开时间和地点的选择、会议的邀请以及会议议程的拟定、会议文件的准备和有关的技术性问题。周密的准备工作可为会议的成功奠定良好的基础。

热身活动
Warming Up

Listen to the recording carefully and answer the following questions.

1. What's the first thing you need to do while preparing a meeting?

2. What should attendees know before they attend the meeting?

3. Why is a written agenda helpful?

4. Why is it so important to plan for a meeting?

示范对话
Model Dialogues

Dialogue 1

A: Hi, Cindy, you have been a secretary for many years in this company. Could you tell me what a secretary should do for a meeting?

B: Well, an important part of the duties of a secretary, I think, is to do well the preparation work for the meeting.

A: What should a secretary do to prepare for a meeting? Could you give me a detailed explanation?

B: First of all, the agenda should be prepared before the meeting. Then you should ensure that those entitled to be present are properly informed.

A: I see, and how about the documents and the information?

B: All the necessary documents and the information relevant to the meeting should be available, preferably printed and distributed before the meeting.

A: And what should a secretary do during the meeting?

B: Of course, she/he should take minutes.

A: And after the meeting?

B: After the meeting, she/he should type the minutes up, and then keep proper records of the business transacted and the resolutions passed, and also implement the decision reached at the meeting.

A: Thank you very much. You are very professional.

B: My pleasure.

Word bank

secretary ['sekrɪt(ə)rɪ] *n.* 秘书；书记；部长

agenda [ə'dʒendə] *n.* 议程；日常工作事项

entitle [ɪn'taɪt(ə)l; en-] *v.* 使……有资格；使……有权利；给……称号

document['dɒkjʊm(ə)nt] *n.* 文件；公文

relevant['relɪv(ə)nt] *adj.* 相关的；切题的；中肯的

distribute [dɪ'strɪbjuːt; 'dɪstrɪbjuːt] *v.* 分配；散布

transact [træn'zækt] *v.* 交易；谈判 *v.* 办理；处理

resolution[rezə'luːʃ(ə)n] *n.* 决议；决心

implement ['ɪmplɪm(ə)nt] *v.* 实施；执行

Notes

1. What should a secretary do to prepare for a meeting?
   秘书要为会议做哪些准备工作呢？

2. First of all, the agenda should be prepared before the meeting.
   首先，要在会前准备好日程安排。

3. Then you should ensure that those entitled to be present are properly informed.
   然后，要确保通知那些有资格参加会议的人员。

4. All the necessary documents and the information relevant to the meeting should be available, preferably printed and distributed before the meeting.
   所有与会议相关的必要文件和信息都应该准备妥当，最好在会前打印好并分发。

5. After the meeting, she/he should type the minutes up, and then keep proper records of the business transacted and the resolutions passed, and also implement the decision

reached at the meeting.

在会议结束后，她/他应该把会议记录打印出来，完好地记录商讨的事宜、通过的决定并执行会上的决定。

Dialogue 2

(It's 9: 00 a.m. Laura, a meeting planner, is coming to the reception office of Good Luck International Hotel to make sure the dinner that will be served tomorrow evening for the meeting is in order. Ada, a staff member of the hotel, is talking with her.)

A=Ada; L=Laura

A: Hello, Laura. Is there anything that I can do for you?

L: Hello, Ada. The meeting is going well and the service you provide is excellent. I just want to make sure that the dinner will be served tomorrow evening.

A: We are pleased that you are satisfied with our service. Don't worry about the dinner. It will be served on time at 7 o'clock tomorrow evening as planned. Do you want to check the menu again?

L: Yes, but I think there will be some changes. I have ordered Western food for our conferees when I booked the meeting, but some of our conferees prefer trying some Chinese food. They think Chinese food is usually very delicious.

A: That's very true. You may change the menu and add some Chinese food.

L: Thank you very much!

A: It's my pleasure. What types of Chinese food do you prefer? Our Chinese restaurant offers a variety of Chinese food — Sichuan food, Cantonese food, Shanghai food, Hunan food, and Jilin food, to name a few.

L: Sichuan food is my favorite.

A: Yes, Sichuan food is delicious, but with spicy taste. I suggest that you should use Cantonese food instead, which is well known for cooking with fresh ingredients. It's light and small in amount.

L: Sounds good. I think our conferees will like it.

A: So you need both Western and Chinese food for your conferees?

L: Sure.

A: We need to change the menu right now.

L: Thank you very much, Ada.

A: You're welcome.

Word bank

staff [stɑːf] *n.* 全体职员；全体员工

conferee [kɒnfəˈriː] *n.* 参加会议者

delicious [dɪˈlɪʃəs] *adj.* 美味的；可口的

menu [ˈmenjuː] *n.* 菜单

variety [vəˈraɪətɪ] *n.* 多样；种类

Cantonese [ˌkæntəˈniːz] *adj.* 广东的 *n.* 广东人；广东话

ingredient [ɪnˈgriːdɪənt] *n.* 原料；要素；组成部分 *adj.* 构成组成部分的

Notes

1. We are pleased that you are satisfied with our service.

您对我们的服务满意，我们感到非常高兴。

2. I have ordered Western food for our conferees when I booked the meeting, but some of our conferees prefer trying some Chinese food.

我已经在预订会议时为参会人员点了西餐，但是有些参会人员想要尝一尝中餐。

3. It is possible for you to change the menu and add some Chinese food.

您可以更改菜单并添加一些中餐进去。

4. Our Chinese restaurant offers a variety of Chinese food — Sichuan food, Cantonese food, Shanghai food, Hunan food, and Jilin food, to name a few.

我们的中餐厅提供很多种中餐——四川菜、广东菜、上海菜、湖南菜和吉林菜等。

5. I suggest that you should use Cantonese food instead, which is well known for cooking with fresh ingredients.

我建议您试试广东菜，它以用新鲜食材原料而闻名。

实用句型
Practical Sentence Patterns

1 The monthly executive committee meeting is planned for the next week. 每月一次的执行委员会会议定于下星期召开。

2 I come to inform you about a meeting scheduled at nine o'clock this morning. 我来通知您今天上午九点有个会议。

3 How long do you expect the meeting to take? 您期望会议开多长时间?

4 Could we possibly rearrange the meeting schedule? 我们可否重新安排会议日程?

5 Shall we postpone the meeting until later in the week? 我们把会议推迟到这周晚些时候,好吗?

6 I'd like to reserve a meeting room for our company. 我想为我们公司预订一间会议室。

7 I wonder if you have any meeting room available for this Friday morning. 我想知道星期五上午是否有空的会议室。

8 I'd like you to make some necessary arrangements for me. 请帮我做一些必要的安排。

9 Please get all things ready and report back to me as soon as you can. 请把一切都准备好,尽快向我汇报。

10 All the necessary documents and the information relevant to the meeting should be available. 所有与会议相关的必要文件和信息都得准备妥当。

11 If there are any problems, I'll be in charge of dealing with them. 如果有什么问题,我将负责处理。

12 It seems that everything is in good order. 似乎一切都秩序井然。

13 We are very glad that you are satisfied with our service. 我们很高兴您对我们的服务感到满意。

14 Do you want to check the menu again? 您想要再核对一下菜单吗?

15 What types of Chinese food do you prefer? 您喜欢什么样的中国食物?

实践实训项目
Practical Training Project

I. Building Up Your Vocabulary

1. Match the words on the left with the best translations on the right.

(1) agenda   a. 有权利

(2) entitle   b. 日程

(3) menu   c. 菜单

(4) document   d. 办理

(5) staff   e. 参会者

(6) ingredient   f. 美味的

(7) conferee   g. 文件

(8) delicious   h. 分配

(9) distribute   i. 配料

(10) transact   j. 全体员工

2. Complete the following dialogue with proper words or expressions.

Z=Mr. Zhou; T=Mr. Thomas

Z: Excuse me, aren't you Mr. Thomas from Australia?

T: Yes. And you are...?

Z: I'm Zhou Feng from Guangdong Import and Export Company.

T: How do you do, Mr. Zhou? _____ (谢谢您来机场接我).

Z: You're welcome. _____(我来帮您拿行李).

T: Oh, thank you very much.

Z: Did you have a good trip?

T: _____(总的来说), it's not too bad.

Z: It's a long way to China, isn't it? _____(我想您一定非常累了).

T: Yes, Exhausted. But I'll be all right by tomorrow and ready for business.

Z: _____(您打算在这里待多久)?

T: About a week.

Z: Good, We'll have enough time for our business talks, _____(如果您感兴趣的话,我们会为您安排一些著名的景点).

T: Wonderful! Nothing would please me more.

Z: But I'm sure _____(您需要好好休息一下) after your long journey. Shall we get into the car and go to the hotel?

T: Exactly! I hope there will be no problem in having one room for one week.

Z: Not at all. _____(我们已经为您预订好了房间).

T: Thanks a lot.

Z: Let's go. This way please.

II. Substitution Drills

Replace the underlined words with the words in the following boxes.

1. Preparing is very important in having a successful <u>meeting</u>.

| conference   convention   session |

2. Follow these steps to help <u>encourage</u> success in your next meeting.

| promote   strive for   lead to |

3. Knowing how to prepare for a meeting is important for all employees and <u>critical</u> for any manager or leader.

| important   crucial   vital |

4. Knowing when not to have a meeting is <u>equally</u> important.

| the same   similarly   fairly   likewise |

5. Decide the <u>type</u> of meeting you are going to have.

| kind   mode   nature |

6. Determine the roles and ask those <u>participants</u> to accept them.

| attendees   conferees   conventioners |

7. Prepare a notice. This should include the date, time, agenda, and <u>venue</u> of the meeting.

| place   spot   site   location |

8. <u>Distribute</u> the notice to the members in good time for the meeting.

| hand out   spread   pass around |

9. Clarify the <u>purpose</u> of the meeting. If you can't figure out what you need to accomplish, you shouldn't be calling a meeting.

| aim   goal   intention   target |

10. Prepare an agenda with the focus <u>stated</u> in a single sentence at the top.

| declared   specified   stipulated   prescribed |

III. Listening Comprehension

Listen to the dialogue and fill in the blanks according to what you hear. Then practice the dialogue with your partner.

A: Miss Wang, the meeting is scheduled for 9: 00 this morning. Have you made the _____?

B: Yes, sir. We'll use the _____ for the meeting.

A: That's fine. The meeting is very important. Where will the guests be received before the meeting begins?

B: In the_____. It's spacious there.

A: We'll have several_____ to attend the meeting.

B: I've arranged for an interpreter to be present. But_____ that these foreign guests could speak Chinese.

A: Yes, I'll try to speak slowly. How do you seat our guests, then?

B: We've prepared name cards to be put on the_____. By the way, what time would you like refreshments to be served?

A: Well, after my report, there'll be an_____for rest and refreshments.

B: All right. I see.

IV. Role Play

Work in pairs or more. Try to act out the following situations.

1. Suppose it is 3: 00 p.m. You are Mr. Zhang. Your meeting is going to be held tomorrow afternoon. You are inspecting the meeting spot now and you find some problems. You want the staff member, Mrs. Liu, to make all the corrections before the meeting and add more flowers. Mrs. Liu is talking with you and promises to make everything done on time.

2. Suppose it is 10: 00 a.m. You are Ada, the planner for the conference at 2: 00 in the afternoon, but now you find some conferees don't have pork. You are worried about it and come to Brown for help. Brown is the manager of the hotel. Brown gives you some suggestions and helps you to deal with the problem.

V. Writing and Speaking

Write one sentence on your own for each of the following words or expressions and speak them out to your partner. Then your partner interprets them into Chinese.

1. an important part

2. the documents and the information

3. goes well

4. be satisfied with

5. booking the meeting

6. well known

Steps on Preparing for a Business Meeting

A well run meeting can be used to effectively train employees, close an important sale, set business goals, and keep major projects on the right track. A successful meeting starts well before everyone is gathered in a conference room. The person running the meeting needs to make arrangements, gather materials, send out invitations, and coordinate the activities. Participants need to be prepared to handle any required tasks, provide feedback, give presentations, or brainstorm ideas. Doing the groundwork ahead of time will keep the meeting running smoothly and help you meet your goals.

Step 1

Determine if you are running the meeting or expected to participate in any fashion. If you are in charge of arrangements, be ready to coordinate scheduling, materials, and the pacing of the meeting.

Step 2

Set a goal for the meeting. Decide if you are trying to make a sale, bring an investor on board, train employees about company policies, or brainstorm new product ideas.

Step 3

Set an agenda for the meeting. Give participants a heads-up if the meeting is expected to be particularly long. Allow time for bathroom or refreshment breaks. Prepare a schedule if there will be multiple speakers or presenters.

Step 4

Make arrangements for a meeting room, conference call, or online meeting. Book a time that works for all key participants. Call or email the group to make sure that the chosen time works for everyone.

Step 5

Send out time and location details to all participants. If you are dealing with employees, let them know if attendance is mandatory or optional. Email conference call-in numbers and codes if you are arranging a phone meeting.

Step 6

Prepare for any needed equipment. For example, if you are going to have a computer presentation, be sure that the conference room has a screen and projector. Know how to hook your laptop up to the projector so that you don't have to waste valuable meeting time dealing with technical details.

Step 7

Take your presentation for a test drive before you do it in front of clients. Make sure your sales or investment pitch is professional, concise, and interesting. Endless charts projected on a screen don't make for compelling meetings. Understand your audience, how you can meet their needs, and what goals you want to reach.

Step 8

Gather materials. Print off handouts. Make sure there are enough chairs for everyone. Prepare refreshments or make catering arrangements if necessary.

Step 9

Remind participants 24 hours ahead, or on the morning of, the actual meeting. Aim to start the meeting promptly at the given time.

Article Source:

http://smallbusiness.chron.com/prepare-business-meeting-454.html

Unit Two

会 议 选 址
Conference Site Selection

 Teaching Targets 教学目标

- To learn how to select an ideal venue for your convention
- To learn to inquire about facilities and services offered by a convention center
- To know the importance of choosing a conference venue
- To improve the listening & speaking skills for convention venue selection
- To master some useful expressions and sentences concerning this topic

背景知识
Background Knowledge

会议能否成功，会址的选择是关键的决定因素之一。一旦会址被选定，即奠定了整个会议的基调。

要举办会议，首先要选择地区和城市，然后选择场馆和设施。根据会议要求的不同，人们会做出不同的选择。一般来说，会议的选址有如下步骤：①初步筛选并确定候选会址名单；②背景调查；③实地考察；④最终选择。

热身活动
Warming Up

Listen to the following materials carefully and answer the following questions.

1. How do you choose the correct meeting venue in terms of space?

2. How do you choose the correct meeting venue in terms of theme?

3. Why should you consider the weather when selecting a venue?

4. Why should you visit the meeting venue?

5. What should you consider when you review the site in person?

示范对话
Model Dialogues

Dialogue 1

Bob, a meeting planner, is conducting an on-site inspection at a convention center. Now he is talking about the convention site with Laura, the sales manager of the convention center.

B=Bob; L=Laura

L: Good morning, sir. How may I help you?

B: Good morning! We are seeking a venue to hold an international convention. So I want to get further information about your center.

L: May I provide some information that might be of interest to you?

B: That will be very nice. I was told that your convention center had extensive experiences of holding international conventions. So, we are expecting to enjoy the services of international standard.

L: You've got a right choice. Look, these are the pictures of past successful conventions we've held before.

B: Wow, that is wonderful! I have more confidence in your convention center now.

L: Thank you. Let me show you around the center and give you a specific introduction to it.

B: It is very kind of you to show me around the convention center. It gives me a great idea of your meeting service facilities.

L: My pleasure. Here is the brochure introducing the details of meeting service at our convention center.

B: Thank you. I will consult with our general manager. And we'll let you know our decision as soon as we can.

L: Thank you for visiting. We are looking forward to seeing you again.

Word bank

on-site [ɒn saɪt] *adj.* 现场的

inspection [ɪnˈspekʃn] *n.* 视察；检查

standard [ˈstændəd] *n.* 标准；水准 *adj.* 标准的；合规格的

extensive [ɪkˈstensɪv; ek-] *adj.* 广泛的；大量的；广阔的

confidence [ˈkɒnfɪd(ə)ns] *n.* 信心；信任；秘密

brochure [ˈbrəʊʃə; brɒˈʃʊə] *n.* 手册，小册子

Notes

1. We are seeking a venue to hold an international convention.

   我们正在寻找举办国际会议的场馆。

2. I was told that your convention center had extensive experiences of holding international conventions.

   我听说贵会议中心在举办国际会议方面有丰富的经验。

3. So, we are expecting to enjoy the services of international standard.

   所以，我们期待享受国际水准的服务。

4. Look, these are the pictures of past successful conventions we held before.

看，这些是我们之前在这里成功举办的会议的图片。

5. Let me show you around the center and give you a specific introduction about it.

让我带您参观会议中心，并且具体地给您介绍一下。

Dialogue 2

Alice(i.e. A) is the PCO; Martin(i.e. M) is the marketing manager of the convention center.

M: Welcome to our center again! I've got your request for bids, and I am sure we can meet your requirements to the utmost.

A: Thank you very much.

M: You are our long-term partner. We will try all means to secure your requirements although it is the peak period.

A: It is kind of you to do the favor for us. But the venue is kind of far away from the downtown area, which is a bit inconvenient for us and the attendees.

M: Well, maybe, but the surrounding here is excellent and spacious. Besides we can offer more parking lots at no charge.

A: That is good. Can you show me around your center?

M: No problem. Let me take you to the function hall first. It has a seating capacity of about 600 people. And the hall illumination is just renovated.

A: Very nice!

M: We also have value-added services to you. We will offer you a package of complimentary items the same as usual.

A: Thanks! By the way, we will still have a group rate this time?

M: No problem! You'll enjoy a discount much lower than the rack rates. Our offer will be more preferential if you use our food and beverage service.

A: I know what you mean. To be honest, the meeting facilities and the staff of the center left me a good impression.

M: Thank you! Then I will draft a contract for your perusal after getting your fact sheet of meeting requirements. It will include all we discussed just now as well as complimentary items we can offer.

A: I am looking forward to it. Thanks for your time.

M: You are welcome.

Word bank

bid [bɪd] *v.* 投标；出价

secure [sɪ'kjʊə; sɪ'kjɔː] *v.* 保护；弄到 *adj.* 安全的；无虑的

peak [piːk] *adj.* 最高的 *n.* 山峰；最高点

surrounding [sə'raʊndɪŋ] *n.* 环境；周围的事物 *adj.* 周围的；附近的

capacity [kə'pæsɪtɪ] *n.* 容量；能力；资格

illumination [ɪˌljuːmɪ'neɪʃən] *n.* 照明；阐明；启发

renovate ['renəveɪt] *v.* 更新；修复；革新

complimentary [ˌkɒmplɪ'mentri] *adj.* 免费赠送的；赞美的

preferential [ˌprefə'renʃ(ə)l] *adj.* 优先的；选择的

perusal [pə'ruːz(ə)l] *n.* 熟读；精读

Notes

1. I've got your request for bids, and I am sure we can meet your requirements to the utmost.

　　我收到了您的询价，而且我确保我们能最大程度地满足您的需要。

2. We will try all means to secure your requirements although it is the peak period.

　　尽管这是高峰期，但是我们会尝试各种办法确保满足您的需求。

3. We also have value-added services to you. We will offer you a package of complimentary items the same as usual.

　　我们也向您提供增值服务。和往常一样我们会向您提供一揽子免费赠品。

4. You'll enjoy a discount much lower than the rack rates.

　　您将享受比市价低很多的折扣。

5. Our offer will be more preferential if you use our food and beverage service.

　　如果您使用我们的餐饮服务，我们的报价会更加优惠。

实用句型
Practical Sentence Patterns

　　1 I want to get more detailed information about your convention center. 我想获得关于贵会议中心的更详细的信息。

2 May I provide you with some information that might interest you? 我可以为您提供一些可能会让您感兴趣的信息吗？

3 I was told that your convention center had a lot of experience of holding conferences. 听说贵会议中心有丰富的举办会议的经验。

4 Let me show you around the center and main conference halls. 让我来带您参观会议中心和主要的会议大厅。

5 It is very kind of you to show me around the convention center. 您能带我参观会议中心，真是太好了。

6 Here is the brochure introducing the details of meeting service at our convention center. 这本小册子介绍我们会议中心的一些会议服务细节。

7 You are our long-term partner. 您是我们的长期合作伙伴。

8 The location is kind of far away from the downtown area. 这儿离市区有些远。

9 We can offer more parking lots at no charge. 我们可以提供更多的免费停车位。

10 Let me take you to the function hall first. 我先带您去功能大厅。

11 It will include all we discussed just now as well as complimentary items we can offer. 它将包括我们刚才讨论的一切以及我们可以提供的免费项目。

实践实训项目
Practical Training Project

I. Building Up Your Vocabulary

1. Match the words on the left with the best translations on the right.

(1) selection	a. 环境
(2) inspection	b. 赠送的
(3) standard	c. 设施
(4) brochure	d. 选择
(5) preferential	e. 检查
(6) complimentary	f. 修复
(7) surrounding	g. 优先的
(8) bid	h. 标准的
(9) renovate	i. 出价
(10) facility	j. 小册子

2. Complete the following dialogue with proper words or expressions.

A: Good morning! This is Beijing _____ (国际会议中心). How may I help you?

B: I am calling from Hong Kong Energy Conservation Association. I wonder if I'd enquire about _____ (举办一场会议) in your center.

A: I am glad to help you, sir. How many people will _____ (参加会议)?

B: A party of 300.

A: _____ (会议将在什么时间举行)?

B: On June 11th and June 12th.

A: Let me have a check, please. Thank you for your waiting, sir. We do have vacant suites and _____ (功能会议厅) during the period you desire for.

B: That is good. Our attendees are all _____ (名流). Is it possible that they each have a suite?

A: Don't worry, sir. Since ours are _____ (五星级) convention center, every attendee is offered a suite and therefore receives a VIP treatment.

B: I like that very much. What is the _____ (房价)?

A: We offer rates competitive with standard hotel rooms, RMB 500 yuan per person per day, including _____ (早茶) and afternoon refreshment.

B: _____ (听起来还不错). We can enjoy low room price and suite service, everybody's dream!

A: Exactly. May I have your name and your _____ (电话号码)?

B: John Lennon. My phone number is 98532166.

A: John Lennon. Your phone number is 98532166. _____ (我马上为您办理).

B: Thank you very much.

A: You are welcome, John. We are looking forward to serving you.

II. Substitution Drills

Replace the underlined words with the words in the following boxes.

1. It is important that you start to look for a <u>venue</u> several months before the date of your event.

place	site	spot

2. For larger events you may even need to start your search at least a year ahead as bigger venues tend to get booked up way <u>in advance</u>.

beforetime	previously	ahead of time

3. The first thing which you need to <u>consider</u> is the amount of attendees you are expecting.

> think about   take into account   take into consideration

4. This will instantly help you to narrow down your list of potential venues as you will be able to <u>disregard</u> those which don't have enough capacity as well as those whose rooms are simply going to be too large.

> neglect   ignore   brush aside

5. The <u>aspect</u> which you have to take into consideration is the budget available.

> point   respect   facet

6. Once you have made yourself a shortlist of potential venues you will need to get more specific in the <u>criteria</u> you require.

> standard   measure   touchstone

7. You will need to work out what sort of venue will <u>complement</u> the theme of your event and also determine whether or not they will have the facilities required for your particular type of event.

> make up for   complete   perfect

8. As the event planner, you should ring round and talk directly with the <u>staff</u> at the venue to see if it meets your list of requirements.

> crew   personnel   clerk

9. Not only will you have to ensure that the facilities meet your requirements but arguably just as <u>vital</u> is the actual location of your venue.

> important   essential   crucial

10. This will be especially important if you are expecting people to travel long distances to <u>attend</u> your event.

> participate in   be present at   take part in

III. Listening Comprehension

Listen to the dialogue and fill in the blanks according to what you hear. Then practice the dialogue with your partner.

Williams(i.e. W) is talking to Jordon(i.e. J) on the phone. Williams who has called to book a conference at Noble Hotel, is an assistant at a culture media company. Jordon is a clerk in Noble Hotel. They have known each other for ages.

W: Hello, this is Williams calling from a culture media company, Shanghai. I called to ask about _____ at Noble Hotel.

J: This is Noble Hotel. _____ ?

W: I am just calling to tell you our company has planned to have a two-day_____ in your hotel. I am wondering if you can do us a favor.

J: It is my pleasure. When will you have your meeting?

W: From July 21st to 26th and there will be 78 people altogether.

J: So, you will stay here for _____ ?

W: Actually, we will finish in the afternoon on the 26th, so we just want to_____ the rooms for five nights.

J: OK. What kind of rooms do you prefer? We have _____, ranging from presidential suites to standard rooms.

W: We need 2 suites and 38 standard rooms.

J: Let me check. 2 suites and 38 standard rooms... OK, we have all of these rooms _____ during the period of your meeting.

W: Also, we need a big meeting hall and a dining room that can_____ 78 people.

J: So a large meeting hall and a dinning hall._____?

W: Oh, we also need a toastmaster capable of _____.

J: All right, that will be no problem. If there is anything else we can help, please let us know_____.

W: OK, thank you. You are_____.

J: My pleasure.

IV. Role Play

Work in pairs or more. Try to act out the following situations.

1. Suppose you are planning an international conference of environmental protection. Having invited 6 speakers, you are now discussing with your partner what kind of format the conference should be organized in.

2. Suppose you are an employee working at a conference center, how will you introduce your center to the attendees?

V. Writing and Speaking

Write one sentence on your own for each of the following words or expressions and speak them out to your partner. Then your partner interprets them into Chinese.

1. detailed information

2. convention center

3. conference hall

4. meeting services

5. peak period

6. downtown area

7. parking lots

8. at no charge

会展之窗
The Window of the Convention & Exhibition

How to Choose a Successful Venue for Your Conference

If you want your event to be a success, you've got to get the venue right. People will only put up with a poor location, difficult transport links, and sub-standard facilities for so long, regardless of how amazing the event is. If you choose a venue that's too big, then your event can come across as under-performing, even if the turnout is as good, or better, than expected. Go too small and everyone feel like they're playing some awful corporate game of sardines. So how do you go about choosing the right venue for your conference?

Know Your Event

Before you rush out looking for a venue, it's incredibly important to get a proper handle on the basics of the event. What's the budget? How many rooms will you need? What kind of footfall are you hoping for? Once you've answered those questions, they can act as a filter, helping you to refine your list of potential venues.

Location, Location, Location

The estate agent's motto works well for event planning too. Think about where the majority of your participants will be coming from. Is your event on a local, regional, or national scale? Come to think of it, and are you going to have any international attendees or guest speakers?

If your event is aimed at pulling in punters from around the country and beyond, then think very carefully about a location in a large city. The transport connections should mean that anyone travelling from outside the local area has a multitude of options open to them.

Is the event held over more than one day? If it is, then you need to think about availability of accommodation across a variety of price points. Not every attendee will want or be able to splash out on a two-night stay at a Park Hyatt or Hilton. It's also a good idea to scope out what the local food and entertainment scene is like. Although many people will want to head back to their hotel for dinner, a shower, and bed, there will be some looking to have a more entertaining evening out.

Nibbles and the Net

Working through the above should have brought you down to a few venues that are suitable. To make that final decision, take a look at what kind of facilities are on offer at each venue. However, don't just go for the swankiest option. Think about what the needs of your conference or event are and find the best fit.

What kind of on-site catering do you need? Just a buffet or a more formal dinner? Can the venue provide this or are you going to have to book a catering service from another place? Of course you need to think about how this might affect your budget.

Also, given that everyone is hooked up to the Internet virtually 24/7 these days via smart phones or tablets, does the venue have a WiFi network, and can it take the strain of hundreds, maybe thousands of people using it simultaneously?

One other thing to bear in mind is whether or not the venue has technical equipment you may need. If you have ushers and on-site support staff, they will probably need walkie-talkies to make communication quick and easy, but will you have to hire a set? And what about tills and debit card terminals for processing payments and tickets?

Hopefully by taking all the above points into consideration, you should be able to find your perfect venue. If you get these areas right, and you've put together a great programme of speakers and events, then you should have a fantastic conference on your hands.

Unit **Three**

会议预订

Booking a Meeting

 Teaching Targets 教学目标

- To learn how to book a meeting
- To know the key factors to consider when booking a meeting room
- To improve the listening & speaking skills for booking a meeting
- To hold conversations concerning this topic

背景知识
Background Knowledge

随着会议产业的发展，各种会议酒店、会议中心也随之发展和壮大起来，为国内外的各种大型研讨会、学术交流、论坛、展览等提供了便利的场所和条件。预订会议是决定要举行会议后的第一个重要步骤。预订会议主要包括确定会议举办时间、选择会址，并最终在相应的酒店或会议中心提前预订。

热身活动
Warming Up

Listen to the recording carefully and answer the following questions.

1. What does "get the most for the money" mean?

2. What should you avoid when booking a meeting?

3. Do all hotels offer the same features and facilities for the meeting rooms?

4. What should be included in the hotel meeting room generally?

示范对话
Model Dialogues

Dialogue 1

Mr. Zhang, who is from Jianghai Environmental Protection Co., Ltd., is calling Suning Universal Hotel to book a meeting. A hotel staff member is answering the phone.

S =staff member; Z=Mr. Zhang

S: Hello. This is Suning Universal Hotel. How may I help you?

Z: Yes, this is Mr. Zhang calling from Jianghai Environmental Protection Co., Ltd. We are going to hold a three-day annual meeting. Can you do us a favor?

S: Yes. Our hotel offers all types of meeting services. When will the meeting start?

Z: It will start from June 7th to June 9th, and our party consists of 60 people. We will be staying for 2 nights.

S: All right. We have lots of guest rooms, including presidential suits, single rooms, and standard rooms. What types of room do you prefer?

Z: We'd like 20 standard rooms.

S: Wait a moment. Let me have a check... Yeah, we do have 20 standard rooms, but unfortunately, they are not all on the same floor.

Z: That's OK. We also need to reserve a dining room equipped with 6 tables for dinner.

S: OK. We have different sizes of dining rooms. The Crystal Room is big enough for 60 people.

Z: On June 8th and June 9th, we also need 6 small meeting rooms, each for 18 people, if they are available. How much does it cost to rent those rooms?

S: We charge $200 per day for the small-size meeting rooms with free tea during the meeting.

Z: Do you provide any meeting facilities during the time?

S: Yes, but the facilities only include a podium, loudspeakers, a smart board, high-speed Internet, and microphones.

Z: So, there is no computer in the room.

S: No, I'm afraid not. You have to pay for using a computer if you really want us to provide one.

Z: OK. We will bring our own.

S: If you need any more detailed information or if there is any change, please call us. Our telephone number is 043184603001.

Z: OK. Thanks a lot.

S: My pleasure.

Word bank

universal [ˌjuːnɪˈvɜːs(ə)l] *adj.* 普遍的；通用的；宇宙的

annual [ˈænjʊəl] *adj.* 年度的；每年的

consist [kənˈsɪst] *v.* 由……组成；在于；符合

available [əˈveɪləb(ə)l] *adj.* 可获得的；可购得的；可找到的；有空的

podium [ˈpəʊdɪəm] *n.* 平台；讲台

loudspeaker [laʊdˈspiːkə] *n.* 喇叭；扬声器；扩音器

microphone [ˈmaɪkrəfəʊn] *n.* 扩音器；麦克风

Notes

1. We are going to hold a three-day annual meeting.

我们打算举行一场为期三天的年会。

2. We have lots of guest rooms, including presidential suits, single rooms, and standard rooms.

我们有很多客房，包括总统套房、单人间和标准间。

3. We also need to reserve a dining room equipped with 6 tables for dinner.

我们还需要预订有6张桌子的晚宴厅。

4. Do you provide any meeting facilities during the time?

您们在会议期间提供任何会议设备吗？

5. Yes, but the facilities only include a podium, loudspeakers, a smart board, high-speed Internet, and microphones.

是的，但是这些设施仅仅包括讲台、扬声器、智能会议平板、高速网络和麦克风等。

Dialogue 2

Revising a Meeting Reservation

Situation: Mr. George, a delegate to the meeting, has booked rooms in Redbuds Hotel. But due to his customer's requests for changes in the booking, he calls the reservations again to alter his booking.

S =staff member; G=Mr. George

S: Good morning. This is Redbuds Hotel. Can I help you?

G: Good morning. I'm calling to revise the reservation we made yesterday.

S: Can you tell me who has made the reservation, please?

G: Our assistant Li Feng.

S: Just hold on please, sir... Yes, I can see it. How would you like to change it?

G: Our customer wants to have deluxe singles instead of standard singles, if possible.

S: One moment, please. Yes, deluxe singles are available. I'll upgrade twenty standard singles to deluxe rooms. May I have your name, please?

G: My name is George Lee.

S: What is your telephone number?

G: 65358867, extension 325.

S: That's 65358867, extension 325. Are there any other changes, Mr. Lee?

G: No, so far so good.

S: OK, let me confirm the details with you. You've reserved twenty deluxe singles and 10 twin-bedded doubles for three nights. The changes and cancellation were made by Mr. Lee. And your confirmation number is C53291.

G: Yes, sorry to have caused you such a trouble.

S: Not at all. I'm always at your service.

Word bank

delegate ['delɪgət] v. 委派……为代表 n. 代表

reservation [rezə'veɪʃ(ə)n] n. 预约，预订；保留

revise [rɪ'vaɪz] v. 修正；复习；校订 n. 修订；校订

deluxe [də'lʌks] adj. 高级的；豪华的

extension [ɪk'stɛnʃən] n. 延长；延期；扩大；伸展；电话分机

confirm [kən'fɜːm] v. 确认；确定；证实；批准；使巩固

cancellation [ˌkænsə'leɪʃ(ə)n] n. 取消；删除

Notes

1. Good morning. I'm calling to revise the reservation we made yesterday.

早上好，我打电话来是想要更改昨天的预订。

2. Our customer wants to have deluxe singles instead of standard singles, if possible.

我们的客户想要豪华单人间，而不是标准单人间，如果可以的话。

3. Yes, deluxe singles are available. I'll upgrade twenty standard singles to deluxe rooms. May I have your name, please?

是的，有豪华单人间。我会把20个标准单人间升级为豪华单人间。可以告诉我您的姓名吗？

4. Let me confirm the details with you. You've reserved twenty deluxe singles and 10 twin-bedded doubles for three nights.

让我来和您确认一下详细信息。您预订了20个豪华单人间，10个双床位双人间，住3晚。

5. I'm always at your service.

乐意为您效劳。

实用句型
Practical Sentence Patterns

① When will your meeting be held? 您们的会议什么时候举行?

② I want to know if you could help us to solve this problem. 我想知道您能否帮助我们解决这个问题。

③ If you need further information, please notify us. 如果您需要进一步的信息，请通知我们。

④ I'll confirm your reservation. 我将确认您的预订。

⑤ We are going to have a three-day annual meeting. 我们将举行一场为期三天的年会。

⑥ Do you provide any meeting facilities during the time? 会议期间您们提供任何会议设施吗?

⑦ Is there a room tonight? 今天晚上有空房吗?

⑧ Do you have a room with a nice lake view? 您们有没有能看到湖景的房间?

⑨ I want a room on a higher floor. 我要一个较高层的房间。

⑩ The room costs 50 dollars a night. 这个房间一晚50美元。

⑪ I will take the room for 5 days. 我将住5天。

⑫ Does this rate include breakfast? 这个费用包括早餐吗?

⑬ I would like to change the room to a double, not single. 我想换成双人房，而不要单人房。

⑭ What's your expected date of arrival? 您预计什么时候到?

⑮ We have no vacancies tomorrow. What about the day after tomorrow? 我们明天已没有空房，后天的怎样?

⑯ We accept Visa and other major credit cards. 我们接受Visa及其他主要的信用卡。

⑰ I really appreciate your help. 我真的很感激您的帮助。

⑱ The rate of the rooms varies from 90 dollars to 900 dollars. You can choose whatever you like. 房间价格不等，从90美元到900美元，任您选择。

实践实训项目
Practical Training Project

I. Building Up Your Vocabulary

1. Match the words on the left with the best translations on the right.

(1) universal		a. 自助餐	
(2) buffet		b. 升级	
(3) consist		c. 取消	
(4) podium		d. 分机	
(5) loudspeaker		e. 包括	
(6) delegate		f. 全球的；普遍的	
(7) deluxe		g. 讲台	
(8) extension		h. 豪华的	
(9) cancellation		i. 扬声器	
(10) upgrade		j. 代表	

2. Complete the following dialogues with proper words or expressions.

Dialogue A

A: Hello, I booked the _____(会议室) today.

B: Hello, Mr. Jordon. Everything is ready for you.

A: Thanks. People should arrive _____(一小时之内).

B: Let me show you our facilities. The meeting rooms are _____(通过这里).

A: OK. Can we have some _____(茶点)?

B: Yes, of course. _____(我们将提供茶和咖啡). We'll serve it through here in the bar.

A: I see.

B: We will also provide some mid-morning _____(零食和蛋糕).

A: That's good. What about lunch?

B: _____(自助餐) will be served at 11: 30 in the restaurant.

A: Great. Do you have _____(网络接口) in the meeting rooms?

B: Yes, we have wireless Internet access in the hotel. You can also use our _____(商务中心) if you need to make photocopies.

A: That's good.

B: Do you have any other questions?

A: No, I think that's everything.

Dialogue B

A: Hello, this is Lisa calling from the Haymarket Media Group, Bingjing. I called to ask about _____(举行会议) at Noble Hotel.

B: Yes. This is Noble Hotel. _____(我能为您做什么)?

A: I'm just calling to tell you our company is going to have an _____(年会) in your hotel. I am wondering if you can help us.

B: _____(这是我的荣幸). When will the conference be held?

A: There will be 80 people _____(参加) the meeting from the 23rd to the 28th in June.

B: So, you'll stay here for six nights?

A: Actually, we will finish in the afternoon on the 28th, so we just want to book those rooms for five nights.

B: OK. _____(您要预订哪类房间)? We have various kinds of rooms, ranging from presidential suits to standard rooms.

A: We need one suit and thirty-nine _____(标准房间).

B: Let me see, one suit and thirty-nine standard rooms... Ok, we have all of these rooms available during the _____(会议).

A: Also, we need a big meeting hall and a _____(餐厅) that can accommodate 80 people.

B: So a large meeting hall and a dining hall. Anything else?

A: Oh, we also need a _____(宴会主持人) capable of speaking both English and Chinese.

B: No problem. If there is anything else we can do for you, please let us know as soon as possible.

A: OK, thank you. _____(谢谢您的帮助).

B: My pleasure.

II. Substitution Drills

Replace the underlined words with the words in the following boxes.

1. When you create a meeting request in Outlook, it is <u>typical</u> and convenient to include the meeting location for the meeting or event.

| proper | distinctive | representative | characteristic |

2. You can use the address book to find a <u>meeting</u> room.

conference   convention   session

3. In the subject box, type a <u>description</u> of the meeting or event.

specification   explanation   illustration

4. Add all the <u>intended</u> invitees to the Tobox.

willing   desired   prospective

5. In both cases, the room's button is not <u>displayed</u> until you add at least one other person.

shown   exposed   revealed

6. It makes the <u>appointment</u> into a meeting request.

nomination   designation   indication

7. To change an appointment to a meeting request, on the appointment tab, in the show group, click <u>scheduling</u> assistant.

planning   arranging   dispatching

8. If the room is <u>free</u>, it will automatically accept your meeting.

available   vacant   spare

9. If the room has already been <u>booked</u>, it will automatically decline the meeting.

reserved   ordered   not available

10. Of course, you would not want all the attendees to be in a crowded room, as this will greatly <u>affect</u> the ambiance of the meeting.

influence   have an effect on   impact on

III. Listening Comprehension

Listen to the dialogue and fill in the blanks according to what you hear. Then practice the dialogue with your partner.

A: My name is George Black calling from the_____. I'd like to reserve rooms for my group.

B: What rooms do you prefer?

A: We have 50 people. Twenty-five_____with a bath please.

B: For which dates, Mr. George?

A: From Feb. 23rd to 25th.

B: Please _____. Twenty-five TWBs for Feb. 23rd to 25th. Yes. We still have those rooms available.

A: Then how much do you charge?

B: Six hundred yuan RMB, _____ 75 U.S. dollars.

A: Fine. _____ . May we use the hotel meeting room during our stay in your hotel? We are going to have a meeting on Feb. 23rd, from 2: 00 p.m. to 4: 00 p.m.

B: No problem. We can make it for you, but we_____ per hour for the use of the hotel meeting room.

A: Oh, I see. _____?

B: There is a 15 percent discount. And we'll send you a _____ by email within five days. May I know your _____?

A: My email address is 7873689@qq.com.

B: Thank you, Mr. Black.

IV. Role Play

Work in pairs or more. Try to act out the following situations.

1. Suppose it is 8: 00 in the morning. You are Mr. Liu, who is responsible for booking a meeting for your company, and you are calling an international standard five-star hotel. When you call up to get some information about booking a meeting, a clerk of the hotel answers the phone and talks about the details with you.

2. Suppose it is 2: 00 in the afternoon. You are Miss Li and you booked a meeting two weeks ago in the hotel. Now you are calling the clerk of the hotel to confirm the specific time of the meeting, the meeting rooms, and so on. A clerk of the hotel answers the phone and confirms the information with you.

V. Writing and Speaking

Write one sentence on your own for each of the following words or expressions and speak them out to your partner. Then your partner interprets them into Chinese.

1. meeting services

2. guest rooms

3. meeting facilities

4. loudspeakers

5. laser pointer

6. slide projectors

7. annual meeting

会展之窗
The Window of the Convention & Exhibition

How to Set up an Efficient and Productive Meeting Room

Every business, no matter how big or small, needs a meeting room where business managers, employees, and partners will talk about important matters. Every aspect of the meeting room matters when conducting a meeting. Ensuring that all necessary equipment is functional and ready to use is very important. To help you out when it comes to setting up a meeting room, here are some important steps you must follow.

Steps

1. Walk around the room. Find the location of all electrical outlets. Devices such as projectors, screens, and computers will need electricity to function, so set up the front of the room where the outlets are positioned. This will help to minimize wires on the floor, which may cause people to fall as they walk around within the room.

Check that cords aren't in the way of people. If needed, tape cords down to the floor to prevent tripping when people walk to their chairs.

2. Check out the size of the space and determine whether it will meet your company's needs. Always bear in mind that the number of attendees will matter when choosing where to set up a functional meeting room. Basically, the smaller the number of attendees, the smaller the space needed; the bigger the number, the larger the space. Of course, you would not want all the attendees to be in a crowded room, as this will greatly affect the ambiance of the meeting.

3. Set up a presentation screen or projector in front, if desired. You must plug in all electrical devices and most importantly, hide all wires under carpets or along the walls.

4. Test to see whether all seats offer an unobstructed view to the front of the room. Generally, the goal is to help all attendees feel that they're a part of the meeting. Avoid the situation of causing anyone to stand just to see what is being presented or discussed at the front. All attendees should feel comfortable, with no hassle in joining in the conversations.

5. Place refreshments and necessary items out. Before the meeting, add bottles of water, pads of paper, and pens on the tables. It is also a great idea to add some fruit.

Unit Four

会议接待与登记

Convention Reception & Registration

 Teaching Targets 教学目标

- To learn to describe on-site registration
- To know both advantages and disadvantages of on-site registration
- To improve the listening and speaking skills for convention registration
- To master some useful words, technical terms, phrases, and key sentence patterns
- To hold conversations concerning this topic

背景知识
Background Knowledge

　　会议登记是与会者参加会议、安排食宿时提供的个人资料等最原始的记载。会议登记也是会议召开前最重要的工作，接待人员要配合会务组做好与会者的登记工作。

　　会议登记可以分为两类：一是预先登记；二是现场登记。会议组织者一般强调并鼓励预先登记。预先登记有助于会议组织者提前掌握出席会议的人数和名单，也便于会务组对客房和餐饮做出安排，还能够减少登记现场的拥挤。少数因特殊原因未能预先登记的人员应在报到时进行现场登记。

热身活动
Warming Up

Listen to the recording carefully and answer the following questions.

1. What's the first step of registration?

2. What if you don't have a personal login?

3. What if you are registering another individual?

4. How soon will you get confirmation?

示范对话
Model Dialogues

Dialogue 1

A: Good morning. Welcome to the Chengdu International Convention Center.

B: Good morning. I'm Mr. Smith from Massachusetts. I am here to attend the Sixth International Convention on Electronics Computer Technology.

A: I see. Have you got your invitation?

B: Yes. Here is my invitation.

A: Let me see. Ah, yes, I found your name on the list. Mr. Smith, professor from Massachusetts Institute of Technology, is that right?

B: Yes. I feel honored to be able to join you in the convention and make a contribution.

A: It is our pleasure. Mr. Smith. Would you please fill in the registration form?

B: Sure. (A few minutes later.) Here you are.

A: Thank you. Here is the meeting packet for you. Please carefully read the materials inside.

B: I will. What a big packet! Now, shall I pay the registration fee here?

A: Yes. 80 dollars, please.

B: Thank you. By the way, I've got some questions to ask you.

A: Yes, please.

B: Do you have a publication plan for the academic papers?

A: Yes, we do have a plan for the excellent academic papers.

B: How can I have my paper published here in China? And how shall I pay for it?

A: It's free of charge. The convention organization committee will choose the best from all the papers delivered and pay for the publication.

B: That's great. Thank you very much.

Word bank

convention [kən'venʃ(ə)n] *n.* 大会；[法] 惯例

electronics [ˌɪlek'trɒnɪks; el-] *n.* 电子学；电子工业

technology [tek'nɒlədʒɪ] *n.* 技术；工艺；术语

invitation [ˌɪnvɪ'teɪʃ(ə)n] *n.* 邀请；引诱

institute ['ɪnstɪtjuːt] *n.* 学会，协会 *v.* 开始(调查)

registration [redʒɪ'streɪʃ(ə)n] *n.* 登记；注册；挂号

material [mə'tɪərɪəl] *n.* 材料，原料 *adj.* 重要的；物质的

academic [ækə'demɪk] *adj.* 学术的；理论的；学院的

publication [pʌblɪ'keɪʃ(ə)n] *n.* 出版；出版物；发表

Notes

1. I am here to participate in the Sixth International Convention on Electronics Computer Technology.

   我来此参加第六届国际电子计算机技术会议。

2. I feel honored to be able to join you in the convention and make a contribution.

   能参加这次会议并做出一点贡献，我深感荣幸。

3. Would you please fill in the registration form?

请您填写一下登记表好吗?

4. Do you have a publication plan for the academic papers?

您有出版学术论文的计划吗?

5. How can I have my paper published here in China? And how shall I pay for it?

我如何才能在中国发表我的论文呢？我怎么付费？

6. The convention organization committee will choose the best from all the papers delivered and pay for the publication.

会议组委会将从所有交付的论文中择优出版并支付出版费用。

Dialogue 2

Cindy(C)= a staff member; Laura(L)=a foreign delegate

C: Hello, welcome to the conference! May I have your name, please?

L : Yes, my name is Laura Brown. I've made an online registration. Is it here for check-in?

C: Yes. Here's the packet with your name badge, programs, abstract booklet, meal coupons, and a convention memento in it.

L: Thanks! Where can I have supper this evening?

C: Oh, you may take part in the welcome reception at 5: 00 p.m. And all the meal times and locations are on the coupons.

L: That's great! By the way, I'm supposed to be a presenter in one of the break-out sessions. I'd like to know where my room is.

C: OK, please let me know your topic, and I will find it for you in the program book.

L: Ah yes! Maybe you can mark off my session on the program. Here it is, on Page 21, right?

C: Yes. It's on the second floor, at the end of the corridor. You may find a conference guide to assist you there tomorrow.

L: But how can I try my PPT for the presentation? Can anyone help me?

C: Take it easy! You can find the technician at your session room this evening, and give it a rehearsal.

L: Super! Then who will chair the session? I've got to get in touch with him or her beforehand.

C: I think you can find your session master at the orientation session at 3: 00 this afternoon. The session is specially aimed to make you first-time attendees familiar with main arrangements of the meeting.

L: Thank you very much! Last question, when can I have the convention proceedings?

C: Oh, yes, that's important. You will receive a CD of the proceedings three weeks after the meeting. Anything else I can help you?

L: Everything is clear so far. Thank you very much for your professional service. Bye bye!

Word bank

badge [bædʒ] *n.* 徽章；证章；标记 *v.* 授给……徽章

program ['prəʊgræm] *n.* 程序；计划；大纲

abstract ['æbstrækt] *n.* 摘要；抽象 *adj.* 抽象的；深奥的

booklet ['bʊklɪt] *n.* 小册子

coupon ['kuːpɒn] *n.* 息票；赠券

memento [mɪ'mentəʊ] *n.* 纪念品；引起回忆的东西

session ['seʃ(ə)n] *n.* 会议；(法庭的)开庭；学期；讲习会

corridor ['kɒrɪdɔː] *n.* 走廊

technician [tek'nɪʃ(ə)n] *n.* 技师，技术员；技巧纯熟的人

rehearsal [rɪ'hɜːs(ə)l] *n.* 排演；预演；练习

orientation [ˌɔːrɪən'teɪʃ(ə)n;ˌ-ɒr-] *n.* 方向；定向；适应

proceeding [prəʊ'siːdɪŋ] *n.* 进行；程序；事项 *v.* 开始；继续做；行进

Notes

1. I've made an online registration.

我已经在网上登记过。

2. Here's the packet with your name badge, programs, abstract booklet, meal coupons, and a convention memento in it.

这是您的资料袋，包括胸卡、计划表、摘要手册、餐券和会议备忘录等。

3. You can find the technician at your session room this evening and give it a rehearsal.

今晚您可以在会议室找到技术人员，然后进行预演。

4. The session is specially aimed to make you first-time attendees familiar with main arrangements of the meeting.

这场会议是专门为您这样的第一次参会的人准备的，目的是让您们熟悉会议的主要安排。

5. Last question, when can I have the convention proceedings?

最后一个问题，我什么时候能获得会议记录？

实用句型
Practical Sentence Patterns

1 I feel honored to be able to join you in the convention and make a contribution. 我很荣幸能够参加此次大会并且做些贡献。

2 Would you please fill in the registration form? 请您填写一下登记表好吗？

3 I've made an online registration. 我已经在线注册过了。

4 All the meal times and locations are on the coupons. 所有的就餐时间和地点都标明在优惠券里。

5 Have you got our official invitation? 您有正式邀请函吗？

6 Please make sure to wear the badges to attend the activities. 请务必佩戴胸卡参加活动。

7 Have you got our invitation? 您带邀请函了吗？

8 Here is your coded badge. 这是您的代表证。

9 Would you please wait a moment? 请您稍等一下好吗？

10 Shall I pay registration fee now? 我现在就要付登记费吗？

11 Have you made pre-registration? 您预先注册了吗？

12 We also offer you the layout map of the convention center. 我们还为您提供会议中心的平面图。

13 We are always at your service. 我们随时为您效劳。

14 I'm sorry to have caused you such trouble. 我很抱歉给您造成这样的麻烦。

15 Here is the convention packet for you. 这是给您的会议资料袋。

16 We look forward to your next participation. 我们期待您下一次参与。

实践实训项目
Practical Training Project

I. Building Up Your Vocabulary

1. Match the words on the left with the best translations on the right.

(1) register   a. 登记

(2) convention   b. 徽章

(3) invitation   c. 摘要

(4) material   d. 餐券

(5) academic   e. 邀请

(6) badge   f. 材料

(7) abstract   g. 会议记录

(8) coupon   h. 学术的

(9) layout   i. 会议

(10) proceedings   j. 布局

2. Complete the following dialogues with proper words or expressions.

Dialogue A

A: Good morning. I'm from Los Angeles Convention Center Project Office. I need to cancel our _____(登记) made Three months ago.

B: I'm afraid it's a pity. The show is drawing near.

A: I'm sorry to have caused you such trouble. We will not be able to attend it_____(由于一些技术原因).

B: That's OK._____ (方便告诉我您的名字吗), please?

A: Lucy Li with Los Angeles Convention Center America.

B: Let me have a check. Well, you have reserved a _____(中央展位) on the second floor, and the booth number is 16, isn't it?

A: All right.

B: _____ (根据条款) specified in the contract, we have to charge 40% of the deposit.

A: Oh, I know it. _____(至少), there will be a 60% refund. Thank you for your service.

B: We _____ (期待) your next participation.

Dialogue B

A: Good morning. _____(请告诉我您们的名字好吗)?

B: The names are Mike Jobson and George Brown.

A: Have you both made_____(预先注册)?

B: Yes, we have.

A: Let me check up on the computer. Yes, I got them now. Here are your _____(代表证) and packet containing some_____(会议资料), such as a copy of the agenda for the meeting, meal coupons, reference materials, etc.

B: Could you please offer me _____(市区地图)?

A: It's in the meeting packet. And we also offer you the_____(平面图) of the convention center.

B: Thank you for your consideration.

A: It's my pleasure. We are always_____(乐意为您效劳).

II. Substitution Drills

Replace the underlined words with the words in the following boxes.

1. They do not have to enter their names and credit card numbers four separate times for the registration, hotel, airline, and rental car.

different	respective	sole

2. However, as meetings are growing in size and complexity, people are abandoning the interview technique because it takes too much time and results in long delays at the registration desk.

giving up	deserting	quiting	forsaking

3. The payment of the convention or meeting can be verified automatically and funds can be transferred to your account more quickly.

checked	confirmed	made certain

4. Whether it is pre-registration or on-site registration, with current technology, online registration is playing a more and more popular role.

pop	fashionable	acceptable

5. In other words, your attendees will not fill out any forms by using a pen or pencil.

participants	conventioners	attenders

6. If they do pre-registration, they can simply go online to your organization's website, fill

out the form, and <u>return</u> it to you.

> send...back   give...back   restore

7. If they are on-site, then have computer terminals handy for the attendees to register <u>electronically</u>.

> automatically   by electronic means

8. This method <u>possesses</u> certain advantages.

> has   owns   gets

9. Since the budget is always a challenge, a cost saving is very <u>helpful</u>.

> beneficial   useful   conducive

10. From the attendees' <u>standpoint</u>, if they can register the meeting on the Web, and you also offer links to hotel registration, rental cars, and airline options, they can do all their planning and travel arrangement at the same time, which is more convenient to them.

> opinion   point of view   viewpoint   outlook

III. Listening Comprehension

Listen to the dialogue and fill in the blanks according to what you hear. Then practice the dialogue with your partner.

A: Good morning, sir. Have you paid the registration_____?

B: Sure, I have _____.

A: Can I have your name and your _____, sir?

B: I'm Black from Asia Green Energy Public Company. Here is my _____.

A: Thank you. Let me look it up on the computer.

A: Mike Black. Yes, I've got it. Here is your_____.

B: Thank you.

A: And here is your_____, Mr. Black.

B: What's inside?

A: In each packet, we placed_____ such as a pencil, a copy of the agenda for the meeting, reference materials, meal coupons, and other related items.

B: By the way, could you please offer me a map of the_____ because I'm new here?

A: Don't worry, Mr. Black. If you are not _____with the Convention Center, you may refer to the layout map which is put in the meeting packet.

B: It's very thoughtful of you to do so. Thank you very much.

A: It's my pleasure.

IV. Role Play

Work in pairs or more. Try to act out the following situations.

1. Suppose you are helping an attendee register but you find that some of his online information is wrong. You decide to solve that problem by doing an on-site registration.

2. Suppose you are going to do an online registration. What should you do step by step?

V. Writing and Speaking

Write one sentence on your own for each of the following words or expressions and speak them out to your partner. Then your partner interprets them into Chinese.

1. online registration

2. welcome reception

3. break-out sessions

4. conference guide

5. official invitation

6. convention center

会展之窗
The Window of the Convention & Exhibition

Surviving Open Online Registration: 10 Tips for a Better Experience!

For those looking to attend Comic-Con for the very first time, the Open Online Registration process can seem quite overwhelming. Gone are the days when one could simply walk into the San Diego Convention Center and buy a badge. The popularity of Comic-Con has morphed the face of badge registration over the years, requiring Comic-Con to change the process frequently to keep up with burgeoning technology and demand.

If this is the first time you attempt to buy a Comic-Con badge, we have a few hints and tips that you should be aware of.

1. Do not share your registration code!

Each registration code is good for one entry into the EPIC Registration waiting room. Your code will authorize one browser and one device only. If you share your code with another person or attempt to enter your code on multiple devices, the new device/browser will be authorized and your old session will expire. Your personal registration code can be found under the "Registration Info" tab in your Member ID account, but please remember in this instance — sharing is not caring.

2. Authorize early!

The EPIC Registration landing page will be open for you to authorize your registration code from 7: 00 a.m. to 9: 00 a.m. Pacific Time (PT) on March 15, 2024. If you arrive after 9: 00 a.m., you will not be able to authorize your code and the waiting room will be closed. Remember, it does not matter what time you arrive at the EPIC Registration landing page. Everyone will be sorted into random order after the sale begins, so take your time and enter your registration code about 10-15 minutes before 9: 00 a.m. (PT).

3. Do not refresh!

Refreshing is to the waiting room what kryptonite is to Superman. Once you have secured your place in the waiting room, it is important that you do not refresh your browser or you will be moved to the back of the line. The EPIC Registration system will not behave as expected if you attempt to refresh through any portion of the badge purchase process. It may be tempting, but just don't do it!

4. Do not use your browser's back button!

We've all made mistakes and we've all missed important information that requires us to go "back" a step online, but in the case of Open Online Registration, it is critical that you take your time while registering and do not hit the back button to repair any mistakes. In multiple rounds of online registration testing, using the back button has produced the greatest number of errors. Comic-Con and EPIC Registration simply cannot stress this tip enough. Using the back button at any point during the registration process could potentially cause the system to error out or release your badges back into inventory. Remember and memorize: back is bad!

5. No Member ID = no badge!

Everyone who wishes to purchase a badge for Comic-Con must have their own valid and confirmed Member ID. This means that you cannot buy a badge for a friend, spouse, child, or parent using your own Member ID. If you are buying badges for others, you will need their personal Member ID and last name.

6. Take a cue from Batman and always be prepared!

In the days leading up to Open Online Registration it is important that you get all of your information ready. You will need your registration code, Member ID, last name, and all of your credit card information at your fingertips. You will also need the Member ID and last name for anyone you are purchasing a badge for. We strongly suggest that you get all of this information ready ahead of time, and check it against the information found on the "Registration Info" tab of your Member ID account.

7. Be tech ready!

Your browser should have Javascript and cookies enabled to function reliably with the EPIC Registration waiting room. These features are usually enabled in the default configuration of most modern Web browsers. If you do not have these features enabled, it is possible that the waiting room application will not function properly. We also recommend that you use one of the following browsers: Firefox, Google Chrome, Internet Explorer, and Safari. We cannot guarantee your results if you use a browser not listed here. The EPIC Registration system is not formatted for mobile devices. Finally, we recommend that you adjust or turn off your computer's power saving setting so that your computer does not go to sleep or power down while in the waiting room.

8. Stock up on snacks!

If all goes well, we anticipate that Open Online Registration will last about an hour. You may have to wait up to an hour for your registration session to begin. You will not be able to see your place in line, so it is important that you pay close attention to your waiting room session. EPIC will automatically refresh the waiting room for you every 120 seconds, and will post live status updates to let you know when badge inventory is running low. Additionally, there will be a blue spinning circle that indicates your page is active. We find that having a nice, refreshing beverage and some protein-packed snacks will help keep you powered through the anxious wait.

9. Relax and take a deep breath!

10. Unfortunately not everyone who participates in Open Online Registration will be able to purchase a badge.

Gaining admittance to the waiting room does not guarantee you a badge or a registration session; there are simply far more people who want to attend than the number of badges available. We appreciate your continued support and hope the new changes we made this year will make the process less problematic than it has been in the past.

Unit Five

会议室布置及会议设施
Conference Room Setup & Meeting Facilities

Teaching Targets 教学目标

- To learn about the commonly used meeting facilities & equipment
- To learn to describe the basic functions of these facilities & equipment
- To know how to set up a meeting room
- To hold conversations concerning this topic

背景知识
Background Knowledge

会场布置对会议效果有很大的影响。布置会场时除了要确保整洁、安静、明亮、通风、安全之外，还应考虑会场形状、大小和桌椅安排等。小型会议可安排在一般会议室，会议室有方形、长方形、圆形、椭圆形等。大中型会议则安排在会议厅，扇形会议厅比长方形的效果更好。

会议设备是指召开会议所需的一系列电子设备，包括影音系统设备、办公系统设备、翻译设备、记录设备、灯光设备等，具体设备有会议系统主机、会议话筒、中央控制系统主机、矩阵切换器、扩音功放、音箱、视频跟踪摄像头、电脑等。

热身活动
Warming Up

Listen to the recording carefully and answer the following questions.

1. Why is proper space planning necessary?

2. How many styles does the room layout have?

3. What is the "presenter style"?

4. What is the "break-out meeting"?

5. What is the classroom-style layout?

示范对话
Model Dialogues

Dialogue 1

B(=Mr. Brown), the organizer of the meeting, is talking about the meeting facilities with Jane, a staff member. Jane=J.

B: Today's topic is about the meeting facilities & equipment. Generally speaking, a list of available facility services and equipment is needed early in the planning process, because the availability or lack of required facilities & equipment impacts on the overall meeting budget. However, the facility's inventory changes frequently due to losses and breakages of the facilities & equipment, so, what should we do?

J: I suggest that we should get the latest information of the facilities & equipment every day.

B: Your idea sounds reasonable. So an updated inventory is needed before completion of final plans.

J: I have a question. What are the so called meeting facilities?

B: Well, the meeting facilities refer to those items for setting up meeting rooms, such as tables, table cloths, chairs, lecterns, and platforms. Most conference centers have their own registration counters, whiteboards, easels, projectors, and screens or smart boards.

J: Do all the convention halls provide all the meeting facilities?

B: Most of them do provide the basic facilities. Besides, sometimes, they can also offer some audio-visual services, standard in-house lighting, Internet connections, and normal air-conditioning. Later on, I will introduce you to the standard facilities in detail.

J: Thank you very much for your information.

B: You are welcome.

Word bank

facility [fə'sɪləti] *n.* 设施；设备
process ['prəʊses] *v.* 处理；加工 *n.* 过程；进行
overall ['əʊvərɔːl] *adj.* 全部的；全体的
inventory ['ɪnv(ə)nt(ə)rɪ] *n.* 存货，存货清单；详细目录
breakage ['breɪkɪdʒ] *n.* 破坏；破损
update [ʌp'deɪt] *v.* 更新；校正，修正 *n.* 更新；现代化
lectern ['lekt(ə)n; -tɜːn] *n.* 讲台；诵经台
easel ['iːz(ə)l] *n.* 画架；黑板架
projector [prə'dʒektə] *n.* 投影仪；放映机

Notes

1. Generally speaking, a list of available facility services and equipment is needed early in the planning process, because the availability or lack of required facilities &

equipment impacts on the overall meeting budget.

通常来讲，在策划过程早期就需要一份可用设施服务与设备清单，因为所需设施与设备是否可用会影响整个会议预算。

2. However, the facility's inventory changes frequently due to losses and breakages of the facilities & equipment, so, what should we do?

然而，设备库存经常由于损失和毁坏而改变。那么，我们应该怎么做呢？

3. I suggest that we should get the latest information of the facilities & equipment every day.

我建议我们应该每天掌握设施与设备的最新信息。

4. Most conference centers have their own registration counters, whiteboards, easels, projectors, and screens or smart boards.

大多数会议中心都有自己的登记台、白板、板架、投影仪，以及屏幕或智能会议平板。

5. Besides, sometimes, they can also offer some audio-visual services, standard in-house lighting, Internet connections, and normal air-conditioning.

此外，有时他们也提供一些视听服务、标准的内部照明、网络连接和正常的空调系统。

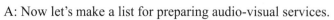
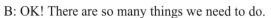

Dialogue 2

A: Now let's make a list for preparing audio-visual services.

B: OK! There are so many things we need to do.

A: Yes. Can you name some of them?

B: Of course! We need to set up the audio and video system, including a Hi-Fi sound system, loudspeakers, a projector, a projection screen, multi-media, and simultaneous interpretation. Besides, we provide one corded microphone and one overhead projector within the meeting room rental.

A: Absolutely right. But, what if anything goes wrong with the equipment?

B: In emergencies like this, we should call in our technician for help.

A: Good.

B: In fact, an in-house technician is always ready to help for the emergencies when the conference is going on.

A: What should we do in case of fire?

B: You can use the extinguisher in case of fire. We will probably come across various kinds of emergencies, such as fire, explosion, stampede, earthquake, etc. The most important thing for us is to keep cool-minded, and then take corresponding measures timely.

A: I've learned a lot from you. Thanks for your professional expression.

B: You are welcome.

Word bank

audio-visual [ɔ: diəu'viʒuəl] *adj.* 视听的；视听教学的

simultaneous [ˌsɪm(ə)l'teɪnɪəs] *adj.* 同时的；联立的；同时发生的

emergency [ɪ'mɜːdʒ(ə)nsɪ] *n.* 紧急情况；突发事件 *adj.* 紧急的；备用的

technician [tek'nɪʃ(ə)n] *n.* 技师，技术员

extinguisher [ɪk'stɪŋgwɪʃə; ek-] *n.* 灭火器；消灭者

explosion [ɪk'spləʊʒ(ə)n; ek-] *n.* 爆炸；爆发；激增

stampede [stæm'piːd] *n.* 惊跑；人群的蜂拥；军队溃败 *v.* 蜂拥；逃窜

corresponding [ˌkɒrɪ'spɒndɪŋ] *adj.* 相当的；相应的 *v.* 类似

Notes

1. We need to set up the audio and video system, including a Hi-Fi sound system, loudspeakers, a projector, a projection screen, multi-media, and simultaneous interpretation.

我们需要建立视听系统，包括高保真音响设备、扬声器、投影仪、投影屏、多媒体和同声传译。

2. In emergencies like this, we should call in our technician for help.

对于这种突发情况，我们应该找技术师来帮忙。

3. In fact, an in-house technician is always ready to help for the emergencies when the conference is going on.

事实上，内部技术师随时准备处理会议进行过程中的突发事件。

4. We will probably come across various kinds of emergencies, such as fire, explosion, stampede, earthquake, etc.

我们很可能会遇到各种各样的突发事件，比如火灾、爆炸、踩踏和地震等。

5. The most important thing for us is to keep cool-minded, and then take corresponding measures timely.

对我们来说最重要的事情就是保持冷静，并及时采取相应措施。

实用句型
Practical Sentence Patterns

① We should get the latest information of the facilities & equipment every day. 我们应该每天获取有关会议设施和设备的最新信息。

② What are the so called meeting facilities? 所谓的会议设施是指什么?

③ Do all the convention halls provide all the meeting facilities? 所有的会议大厅都提供完备的会议设施吗?

④ I will introduce you the standard facilities in detail. 我将详细地为您介绍关于标准设施的情况。

⑤ A convention center has air walls to divide the space to fit the need of the meeting. 会议中心有活动隔断,可以根据会议的需要来分隔场地。

⑥ The break-out area may be common area so that the break items can be shared among the various groups. 分隔区为公共区域,这样,隔断物可以由不同的团体共享。

⑦ I'll check if there are enough chairs, and if the lighting and air-conditioning are all right. 我将检查是否有足够的椅子,以及照明和空调是否都没有问题。

⑧ And please get some water, glasses, and ashtrays ready as well. 另外,也请把水、杯子和烟灰缸准备好。

⑨ Will you need any additional equipment set up for your speech? 您演讲时需要其他设备吗?

⑩ We don't want any big problems. 我们不想有任何大差错。

⑪ Do you need any overhead projector? 您需要投影仪吗?

⑫ Besides, we also offer some audio-visual services, standard in-house lighting, Internet connections, and normal air-conditioning. 除此之外,我们还提供一些视听服务、标准内部照明、网络连接和标准的空调。

⑬ More importantly, we should pay attention to the quality, type, or size of the equipment. 更重要的是,我们应该重视设备的质量、类型或尺寸大小。

⑭ What if anything goes wrong with the equipment? 如果设备出问题了,怎么办呢?

⑮ In emergencies like this, we should call in our technician to help. 在这种紧急情况下,应该叫我们的技术人员来帮助解决。

⑯ Choosing the best equipment for your meeting is simple and doesn't have to take a lot of time. 为您的会议选择最好的设备其实很简单,不需要花费很多时间。

实践实训项目
Practical Training Project

I. Building Up Your Vocabulary

1. Match the words on the left with the best translations on the right.

(1) layout   a. 技师

(2) inventory   b. 扬声器

(3) update   c. 库存

(4) lectern   d. 灭火器

(5) projector   e. 烟灰缸

(6) technician   f. 讲台

(7) extinguishor   g. 布局

(8) loudspeaker   h. 投影机

(9) ashtray   i. 更新

2. Complete the following dialogue with proper words or expressions.

A: Good morning, Bob. Thank you for giving us a chance to present our _____(提议).

B: You are welcome. You deserve it. You have been doing _____(许多工作).

A: Thank you. Here is our proposal.

B: What are you proposing?

A: First of all, we can train_____(专业的) hostesses for you. We could improve the _____(沟通技巧) of your staff.

B: That sounds great!

A: Besides, we can provide services like distribution of promotional booklets and samples, marketing products,_____(安排会议), finding contacts, and organizing games and competitions.

B: That is good. Could you provide bilingual switchboard operators and _____(秘书服务)?

A: Sure. These are _____(基础服务) we offer. In addition, we can offer management of schedules, meeting rooms, mail sorting, _____(旅行预订), and distribution of badges.

B: That is what we expect.

A: After the event, we also provide detailed reports and_____(回馈) to you.

B: Good. Let me read your proposal first. I will contact you very soon.

II. Substitution Drills

Replace the underlined words with the words in the following boxes.

1. Every business, no matter how big or small, needs a meeting room where business managers, employees, and partners will talk about important matters.

| things | issues | topics |

2. Ensuring that all necessary equipment is functional and ready to use is very important.

| facilities | furniture | articles |

3. All attendees should feel comfortable and be able to join in the conversation without any hassle.

| difficulty | trouble | headache |

4. If needed, tape cords down to the floor to prevent tripping when people walk to their chairs.

| stumbling | falling over | tumbling |

5. Check out the size of the space and determine whether it will meet your company's needs.

| decide | make up one's mind | find out | make sure |

6. Always bear in mind that the number of attendees will matter when choosing where to set up a functional meeting room.

| participants | conferees | comers |

7. Basically, the smaller the number of attendees, the smaller the space needed.

| fundamentally | essentially | in essence |

8. Of course, you would not want all the attendees to be in a crowded room, as this will greatly affect the ambiance of the meeting.

| highly | extremely | badly | quite |

9. Set up a presentation screen or projector in front, if desired.

| necessary | wanted | needed | expected |

10. You must plug in all electrical devices and most importantly, hide all wires under carpets or along the walls.

| equipment | apparatus | parts |

III. Listening Comprehension

Listen to the dialogue and fill in the blanks according to what you hear. Then practice the dialogue with your partner.

A: There will be an _____ to be held in a week. We need to make a list of facility services and equipment.

B: OK! Let's start with that.

A: First of all, let me_____ again, we should pay more attention to the audio-visual system and check it again and again soon later.

B: No problem.

A: How about the_____ and loudspeakers?

B: I've got them ready. I've also checked all the other_____ aids and speaker's podium.

A: Have you prepared some pencils and notepads for the_____?

B: Certainly. All the items needed are included in the_____.

A: Have you informed the_____ of several hostesses ushering the participants?

B: Yes. I've also sent each speaker a_____ personally.

A: Good. You did an excellent job.

B: Thank you for your_____.

IV. Role Play

Work in pairs or more. Try to act out the following situations.

1. Suppose you are an organizer of a conference and you find a microphone broke down just before a speech begin. After immediately sending for technicians, which may take a while, how can you explain to the audience and fill in the gap?

2. Suppose you are an organizer of an international conference, how do you communicate with the on-site attendees?

V. Writing and Speaking

Write one sentence on your own for each of the following words or expressions and speak them out to your partner. Then your partner interprets them into Chinese.

1. meeting facilities

2. convention halls

3. air walls

4. air-conditioning

5. overhead projector

6. Internet connections

会展之窗
The Window of the Convention & Exhibition

Conference Arrangement Tips

Arranging for a conference efficiently and effectively can leave attendees with a positive image of you, your company, and any conference organizers involved. On the contrary, if you get one major aspect of the conference wrong such as not providing enough seating, the reputation of all involved could be impaired.

Arrange a conference using proven techniques and you can walk away from the event with complements and perhaps even a promotion.

Location

Carefully select the conference location. Consider how far away the location is for attendees and how accessible the location is from a transportation perspective. Are airports nearby? How accessible is public transportation? Will a sufficient number of hotel rooms be available?

Budget

Prepare a budget for the conference and build in a contingency for unexpected expenses. According to the Ontario Convention and Visitors Bureau, budget items would include food and beverages, service charges, decorations, entertainment, speaker transportation and fees, meeting room and equipment rentals, printing, security, booth setup, and printing.

Online Registration

Use online registration because it is convenient for those registering and provides you with the fastest feedback on who has registered. In addition, Internet registration can save up to 90 percent of time compared to off-line methods of handling registration.

Negotiate

Do not assume published prices are the prices you will have to pay for services to support the conference, recommends the Hospitality Net. For example, in the case of hotel rooms, you can often get a discount if a block of rooms are all reserved at the same time.

Engage Attendees

Ask the attendees to actively participate in the event. For example, ask attendees to share their own experience and ideas during a presentation. For one session, organize a round table of attendees and experts to interact.

Article Source:

http: //www.ehow.com/info_7737147_conference-arrangement-tips.html

Unit Six

开幕式和闭幕式

Opening & Closing Ceremony

 Teaching Targets 教学目标

- To learn to understand opening and closing ceremony
- To know the importance of opening and closing ceremony
- To grasp some useful words, phrases, and key sentences related to the topic
- To hold conversations concerning this topic

背景知识 Background Knowledge

开/闭幕式(Opening/Closing Ceremony)是宣布各种会议活动正式开始或结束的具有象征性和标志性的仪式。开/闭幕式的形式主要有两种：一种是以致辞为主的形式；另一种是文艺晚会的形式。开/闭幕式程序包括介绍出席仪式的领导人和主要来宾、致开/闭幕词、升国旗或会旗、奏国歌或会歌、代表致辞、剪彩、参观、颁奖、表演等。

热身活动 Warming Up

Listen to the recording carefully and answer the following questions.

1. What kind of opening speech do you think it is?

2. Who is the speaker?

3. What does the speaker want to tell the audience?

4. What is the hard problem according to the speaker?

5. How do you solve the problem in your opinion?

示范对话 Model Dialogues

Dialogue 1

(It is the very beginning of the opening ceremony of International Conference on Global Food Security.)

C=Conference Chair; B=Mr. Blair; S =Dr. Smith

C: Ladies and gentlemen, respected guests, dear friends, good morning. I am Charlie Black. It is my great honor to preside this wonderful ceremony. It is also my great pleasure to warmly welcome you to this International Conference on Global Food Security. According to the agenda, let's welcome Mr. Blair, Chairman of this conference to deliver a welcome speech.

B: Good morning, ladies and gentlemen. On behalf of the Committee of this conference, I wish to warmly welcome all of you to be here and also to offer cordial congratulations on the opening of the 10th International Conference on Global Food Security. I sincerely hope that you have something to share regarding the development of food security industry, and make this conference a worthwhile experience for all concerned. I believe our cooperative efforts are sure to be productive and will contribute directly to further trade expansion to the benefit of our regions. Thank you.

C: We are grateful to Mr. Blair for promoting this conference. As scheduled, now, I am pleased to introduce to you our guest speaker Dr. Smith. Dr. Smith is a great expert in food security industry who has been studying "food security" for several years. Now, let's welcome Dr. Smith to give us a brief speech.

S: Good morning. It is a pleasure for me to be here today. As I look around the conference hall, I find all sorts of products on show which are truly worthwhile to be exhibited here and shared. They certainly reveal the results of our latest technology. I will catch the opportunity to share with you my opinions on the notion of "security".

Word bank

preside [prɪˈzaɪd] *v.* 主持

security [sɪˈkjʊərətɪ] *n.* 安全；保证

agenda [əˈdʒendə] *n.* 议程；日常工作事项

deliver [dɪˈlɪvə] *v.* 交付；发表；递送

cordial [ˈkɔːdɪəl] *adj.* 热忱的；诚恳的

cooperative [kəʊˈɒpərətɪv] *adj.* 合作的；合作社的

contribute [kənˈtrɪbjuːt; ˈkɒntrɪbjuːt] *v.* 贡献，出力；投稿；捐献

notion [ˈnəʊʃ(ə)n] *n.* 概念；见解

Notes

1. It is my great honor to preside this wonderful ceremony.

我很荣幸主持这个美好的典礼。

2. According to the agenda, let's welcome Mr. Blair, Chairman of this conference to deliver a welcome speech.

根据会议议程，让我们欢迎会议主席布莱尔先生致欢迎词。

3. On behalf of the Committee of this conference, I wish to warmly welcome all of you to be here and also to offer cordial congratulations on the opening of the 10th

International Conference on Global Food Security.

我代表本次会议组委会，对大家的到来致以热烈的欢迎，并对第十届全球食品安全国际会议的开幕致以诚挚的祝贺。

4. I believe our cooperative efforts are sure to be productive and will contribute directly to further trade expansion to the benefit of our regions.

我相信我们的合作努力一定会富有成效，并将直接推进贸易的发展，造福我们的地区。

5. As I look around the conference hall, I find all sorts of products on show which are truly worthwhile to be exhibited here and shared.

当我环顾会议大厅，我发现展示的多种产品的确很值得展览和分享。

Dialogue 2

(Paul is a reporter who wants to continue with his report on the result of the International Conference on environment-friendly products. He is in need of the detailed information about the Conference. The operator of the Chengdu Conference Center is answering the phone.)

O=operator; P=Paul Smith; S=staff member

O: Chengdu Conference Center. What can I do for you?

P: Hello. This is Paul Smith, a reporter from Conference & Incentive Travel Magazine. I want to continue with the report on the result of the International Conference on environment-friendly products. I would like to talk to someone in charge of the organization of the conference.

O: Hold on a minute, please. I will put you through to the Organizing Committee.

S: Hello. This is the Organizing Committee. Can I help you?

P: Hello. This is Paul Smith, the reporter calling from Conference & Incentive Travel Magazine. I want to go on with my report on the conference. Would you mind giving me some detailed information concerning the result of this International Conference on environment-friendly products?

S: Sure, Paul Smith. We are ready to provide any convenience for the media. The International Conference on environment-friendly products was opened on June 16th and it is going to be closed tomorrow. So far, the convention has talked about 368 projects and signed about 19 billion U.S. dollars' worth of contracts.

P: Well, the Conference seems to have got a quite positive result. And it's going to be a great success.

S: Absolutely. Its influence has obviously been upgraded than any other time. During the conference, 30 domestic and foreign delegations and 130,000 guests have come.

P: Is it reasonable to predict that the next conference on environment-friendly products will be more thriving and attractive?

S: Probably.

P: Thanks for your professional information. By the way, when will the closing ceremony begin tomorrow?

S: At 4: 00 in the afternoon. We are looking forward to your attendance. There will be several reports from subcommittees at the ceremony.

P: Many thanks.

S: You are welcome.

Word bank

incentive [ɪn'sentɪv] *n.* 激励；刺激 *adj.* 激励的；刺激的

positive ['pɒzɪtɪv] *adj.* 积极的；阳性的；确定的

contract ['kɒntrækt] *n.* 合同，契约 *v.* 收缩；感染；订约

upgrade [ʌp'greɪd] *v.* 使升级；提升 *n.* 升级；上升

domestic [də'mestɪk] *adj.* 国内的；家庭的

delegation [delɪ'geɪʃ(ə)n] *n.* 代表团；授权；委托

predict [prɪ'dɪkt] *v.* 预报；预言

thrive [θraɪv] *v.* 繁荣；兴旺

subcommittee ['sʌbkəmɪtɪ] *n.* 小组委员会；委员会的附属委员会

Notes

1. I would like to talk to someone in charge of the organization of conference.

   我想要和会议组织机构的负责人谈谈。

2. Would you mind giving me some detailed information concerning the result of this International Conference on environment-friendly products?

   您能够对本次环保产品国际会议的结果提供一些详细的信息吗？

3. So far, the convention has talked on 368 projects and signed about 19 billion U.S. dollars' worth of contracts.

   到目前为止，会议讨论了368个项目，并签署了价值约190亿美元的合同。

4. The Conference seems to have got a quite positive result. And it's going to be a great success.

这次会议似乎取得了很积极的结果，并且将会取得很大的成功。

5. Is it reasonable to predict that the next conference on environment-friendly products will be more thriving and attractive?

是否有理由预测下一届环保产品会议会更加欣欣向荣和有吸引力呢？

实用句型
Practical Sentence Patterns

1️⃣ Ladies and gentlemen, distinguished guests, good morning. 女士们，先生们，贵宾们，早上好。

2️⃣ It is my great honor to preside this wonderful opening ceremony. 我很荣幸主持这个精彩的开幕式。

3️⃣ First of all, please allow me to express my heartfelt thanks to all the guests for attending this conference. 首先请允许我向出席今天会议的各位来宾表示衷心的感谢。

4️⃣ I am glad for such a big opening ceremony for the hotel. And welcome all of you to be here. 我很高兴出席这家酒店的盛大开幕式，欢迎大家的到来。

5️⃣ I would like to extend my cordial welcome to all of you. 我谨向各位表示最热烈的欢迎。

6️⃣ It gives us a feeling of special joy to have the opportunity of entertaining our distinguished guests. 我们特别高兴能有机会招待我们的贵宾。

7️⃣ It is my great honor and pleasure to be invited today to share this happy occasion. 今天我非常荣幸、非常高兴地应邀前来与大家分享这幸福时刻。

8️⃣ Now, let's welcome Dr. Smith to give us a brief speech. 现在，让我们欢迎史密斯博士给我们做一个简短的演讲。

9️⃣ I wish this meeting a complete success! 预祝会议圆满成功！

🔟 Before we close today's meeting, let me just summarize the main points. 在我们结束今天的会议之前，让我总结一下要点。

1️⃣1️⃣ Thanks for your participation. 谢谢您的参与。

1️⃣2️⃣ Thank you for your coming. We are looking forward to meeting you again next time! 谢谢您的光临，期待下次再相逢。

1️⃣3️⃣ Wish the conference a complete success. 预祝大会圆满成功！

1️⃣4️⃣ The conference has achieved fruitful results. 本次大会取得了丰硕的成果。

1️⃣5️⃣ I declare the meeting closed victoriously. 我宣布本次大会胜利闭幕。

实践实训项目
Practical Training Project

I. Building Up Your Vocabulary

1. Match the words on the left with the best translations on the right.

(1) ceremony		a. 贡献
(2) preside		b. 总结
(3) agenda		c. 努力
(4) deliver		d. 积极的
(5) contribute		e. 发送
(6) positive		f. 卓著的
(7) domestic		g. 仪式
(8) strive		h. 日程
(9) distinguished		i. 国内的
(10) summarize		j. 主持

2. Complete the following dialogue with proper words or expressions.

A: Am I too late for the_____(开幕式)?

B: No, _____(刚开始). The runner is just coming into Olympic Village with the torch.

A: Oh, _____(真是太激动人心了!) I love the Summer Olympics. Track and field, gymnastics, swimming — I can't wait!

B: Oh, here come the athletes from each country, with their flag bearer in front.

A: Isn't it funny that the country only has one competitor?

B: _____(一点儿都不！) Can you imagine the accolades you'd get as the only athlete from your country that's of Olympic caliber? I'd trade places with her any day.

A: This schedule says that the track and field _____(比赛项目) begin tomorrow.

B: Yeah, but those are just the _____(预选赛) heats. The real races don't start for three days. What's that?

A: My flag. I'm _____(喝彩) on the U.S. team.

B: From the _____(客厅)?

A: Sure, why not? It can't hurt, can it?

II. Substitution Drills

Replace the underlined words with the words in the following boxes.

1. The first paragraph of the speech is <u>perhaps</u> the most important of them all.

| possibly maybe probably likely |

2. It helps the speaker to <u>grab</u> the attention of the audience and try to engage their interest.

| catch attract grip enchain |

3. This can be <u>achieved</u> by raising a thought-provoking question or making a controversial or interesting statement.

| got obtained reached attained |

4. Once the members of the audience are engaged, the speech can move on <u>seamlessly</u>.

| without a seam perfectly successfully |

5. The body is the <u>largest part</u> of the opening ceremony speech.

| main part main body principal part |

6. During this stage, the audience needs to learn to <u>connect</u> with the person presenting the speech and understand every bit of the story.

| associate link combine |

7. The best way to make the body of the speech interesting is to come up with points that are easy to <u>internalize</u>.

| imply interiorize personal subjective |

8. The points should be <u>organized</u> in such a way that any points categorized together are co-related.

| structured unionized arranged |

9. Once that is done, the closing part should <u>summarize</u> the speech, provide food for thought for the listeners, and then end with a final thought or emotion.

| sum up generalize outline |

10. A good opening ceremony speech is written with a <u>structured</u> format of body, content, and closing statements.

| organized integrated methodic |

III. Listening Comprehension

Listen to the dialogue and fill in the blanks according to what you hear. Then practice the dialogue with your partner.

Paul: Hurry up, otherwise we'll miss the _____ of the Track and Field Sports Meeting of our university.

Jack: OK. _____. Let me tie my shoelaces.

Paul: What _____ are you in?

Jack: 100-meter _____, 110-meter hurdle, and 800-meter relay.

Paul: You must be a very _____.

Jack: I'm fond of races. I was on the _____ three years ago.

Paul: Track events require development of the _____. What's your record for the 100-meter dash?

Jack: 11'5. I broke the _____ last year. What events are you in?

Paul: The _____ and high jump.

Jack: What's your record of high jump?

Paul: 2.23 meters.

Jack: Not bad. I'm sure you can get _____ at this sports meeting.

Paul: I do hope so.

IV. Role Play

Work in pairs or more. Try to act out the following situations.

1. Suppose you are the chairman of Skylark Arts Company. You need to make a speech at the closing ceremony of the 6th International Conference on Tourism and Hospitality held at Shanghai International Conference Center.

2. Suppose you are going to settle an agenda for an opening/closing ceremony. What should be listed?

V. Writing and Speaking

Write one sentence on your own for each of the following words or expressions and speak them out to your partner. Then your partner interprets them into Chinese.

1. distinguished guests

2. heartfelt thanks

3. opening ceremony

4. cordial welcome

5. main points

6. fruitful results

会展之窗
The Window of the Convention & Exhibition

How to Give an Award Ceremony Speech

Award shows are known for not only the performances, celebrity outfits, and the glamour, but also the award acceptance speeches. While you may not be attending the Oscars or Grammys any time soon, you may attend an award ceremony at your job, school, or other organization, and be required to give an acceptance speech. A good speech garners respect from the audience, while a bad one may put people to sleep or confuse them.

Decide ahead of time who will speak if multiple people are part of the potentially winning entity. Either pick one person or decide how long each person may speak.

Make a list of every person you need to thank, such as your family, partners, mentors, and other people. You may not have time to thank everyone, so it's okay to sum up groups, such as "my family" or your marketing team at your place of employment.

Say concisely what the award means to you. Show genuine thanks and appreciation, but do so in a few words. Example: "Ever since I started medical school, I knew this award was something to strive for."

Ask someone associated with the award ceremony what the time constraints are for an acceptance speech. If he is unsure of a set time, err on the side of keeping the speech brief, such as a minute or less.

Write out the speech. Do not write out every single word, but instead key remarks and people to thank. Type the speech and print it in a font that's large and easy to read. Make the speech concise and genuine. Avoid showboating or using the moment as an opportunity to push another agenda or your political views.

Practice your speech multiple times. You may get nervous when presenting the speech, so practicing helps you feel comfortable and not forget your words.

Give the speech at the ceremony, breathing normally and making eye contact with the audience at least every two or three sentences. Speak confidently into the microphone, smile and act thankful, without coming off as cocky.

Article Source:

http://www.ehow.com/how_12102269_give-award-ceremony-speech.html

Unit Seven

会议餐饮服务
Catering Services for Meetings

 Teaching Targets 教学目标

- To learn about the importance of food-beverage services
- To master some useful professional words and expressions on catering services for conventions
- To improve the listening and speaking skills on catering services
- To hold conversations concerning this topic

背景知识
Background Knowledge

一般而言，会议通常统一安排餐饮。餐饮安排通常有两种形式——自助餐或者围桌餐。餐饮类别有中式、西式及清真系列。

对于统一安排餐饮的会议，成本的控制非常重要，自助餐一般可以通过发餐券来控制，可以事先确定餐标及餐谱，严格区分正式代表与随行人员、家属，有特殊要求者可以和餐厅协商。围桌式餐饮安排比较复杂——对于大型会议，尤其如此。围桌式餐饮安排需要考虑的问题有开餐时间、每桌人数、入餐凭证、同桌者安排、特殊饮食习惯者、酒水种类及付款方式等。

热身活动
Warming Up

Listen to the recording carefully and answer the following questions.

1. What does the catering department often fail to do?

2. What is high-quality service dependent on?

3. Why is the initial contact between the customer and staff so important?

4. How do you understand the motto "Reputation first, customer foremost"?

示范对话
Model Dialogues

Dialogue 1

Miss Lucy (i.e. L), a conference organizer, is talking with a guest, Alice (i.e. A), about the food & beverage services.

A: Good morning, Miss Lucy. I know you have already known our schedule, but I would like to check the meal times for tomorrow's forum.

L: Well, breakfast will be served in the banquet hall from 6: 00 to 9: 00. Do you have any special requirements there?

A: We do have a lot of Indians and Italians attending the forum, so I think it would be a good idea to serve Indian food and Italian food, in addition to Chinese food.

L: No problem. Could you please speak more specifically?

A: They prefer breakfast to be traditional, healthy, nutritious, and refreshing. For example, Indian tofu, eggs, vegetarian sausages, pancakes, Swiss roll, coffee, milk, cornflakes, and juice — all of the above will be very nice options.

L: I've got it. Lunch time is from 11: 30 a.m. to 1: 00 p.m. And how about the teatime? Would you like coffee to be served in the lobby?

A: No, I want to try something special. I think Chinese Oolong Tea would be very nice.

L: That is OK and I am sure we can arrange that. Now to accompany the meal, do you want some wine?

A: Do you have any good suggestions?

L: I think that whisky or brandy would be more enjoyable.

A: OK. And we have six vegetarians, that I do know, so pork and shrimps will be out for them.

L: I'll make a note of that.

A: Thank you very much. Now everything is OK.

L: You are welcome. I hope you can have a nice stay here.

Word bank

forum ['fɔːrəm] *n.* 论坛；讨论会

beverage ['bev(ə)rɪdʒ] *n.* 饮料

banquet ['bæŋkwɪt] *n.* 宴会；盛宴

traditional [trə'dɪʃ(ə)n(ə)l] *adj.* 传统的；惯例的

nutritious [njʊ'trɪʃəs] *adj.* 有营养的；滋养的

refreshing [rɪ'freʃɪŋ] *adj.* 提神的；使……清爽的

vegetarian [vedʒɪ'teərɪən] *n.* 素食者；食草动物 *adj.* 素食的

Notes

1. Do you have any special requirements there?

您有什么特别的要求吗？

2. We do have a lot of Indians and Italians attending the forum, so I think it would be a good idea to serve Indian food and Italian food, in addition to Chinese food.

我们确实有很多印度人和意大利人参加论坛，所以我认为除了中国菜，最好提供印度菜和意大利菜。

3. They prefer breakfast to be traditional, healthy, nutritious, and refreshing.

他们喜欢传统、健康、营养和提神的早餐。

4. Now to accompany the meal, do you want some wine?

您想要来些葡萄酒来搭配菜肴吗?

5. And we have six vegetarians, that I do know, so pork and shrimps will be out for them.

据我所知，我们有6位素食者，所以不要为他们供应猪肉和大虾。

Dialogue 2

A: Would you like to try this dish? It is sea urchin. It is very rich in protein, which is very good for people's health.

B: OK, I'll try it.

A: Now, we have the wild boar meat products in the pottery pot.

B: Oh, my god. It must be very lovely.

A: Yes, I believe so.

B: And what is this? (Pointing) Oh, see, I finally see clearly. It's lobster. It is very nutritious.

A: Yes, indeed. It seems that you like sea-food.

B: Yes, why not? I'm not a vegetarian. You know, Chinese food is different from ours.

A: Yes, quite different.

B: We have got so many delicious things tonight.

A: This is the Chinese way of receiving guests. We try to persuade our guests to have more food we prepare for them, and thus show our hospitality.

B: That is wonderful.

A: How do you like the dinner? Is it all right for you?

B: Terrific. Thank you very much for your dinner. I like it very much. This is the best Chinese food I have ever had.

A: It's our pleasure.

Word bank

urchin ['ɜːtʃɪn] *n.* 海胆；顽童，淘气鬼

protein ['prəʊtiːn] *n.* 蛋白质 *adj.* 蛋白质的

boar [bɔː] *n.* 野猪

pottery ['pɒt(ə)rɪ] *n.* 陶器；陶器厂

lobster [ˈlɒbstə] *n.* 龙虾

nutritious [njʊˈtrɪʃəs] *adj.* 有营养的；滋养的

hospitality [hɒspɪˈtælɪtɪ] *n.* 好客；殷勤

Notes

1. It is very rich in protein, which is very good for people's health.

   它蛋白质含量丰富，有益健康。

2. It is very nutritious.

   它很有营养。

3. Yes, why not? I'm not a vegetarian.

   是的。我不是素食者。

4. This is the Chinese way of receiving guests.

   这是中国的待客之道。

5. We try to persuade our guests to have more food we prepare for them, and thus show our hospitality.

   我们会尽力让客人多享用我们为他们准备的菜品，以显示我们的热情好客。

实用句型
Practical Sentence Patterns

1 Would you like something to drink, please? 您想喝点什么？

2 Which brand of beer would you prefer, sir? 您要什么牌子的啤酒，先生？

3 We have a variety of soda water and fruit juice. 我们有各种汽水和果汁。

4 Could I have a few minutes to look through the drink list first? 我能先看看饮料单吗？

5 Excuse me, may I take your plate? 打搅了，我可以把盘子收起来吗？

6 Would you like some dessert? 您要来点儿甜点吗？

7 What sort of table plan do you have in your mind? 您希望餐桌怎么摆放？

8 May I have some toothpicks? 我能要些牙签吗？

9 I've never had any food as delicious as this. 我从未尝过这么好吃的饭菜。

10 I'd like to pay it by credit card. 我想用信用卡付款。

11 How would you like your steak done, sir? Rare, medium, or well-done? 您的牛排要怎么做？要三成熟、五成熟还是全熟？

⑫ What would you like to have for your main course? 主菜您要什么?

⑬ Excuse me, could I have a menu, please? 打扰一下,请给我菜单好吗?

⑭ Is there anything special you'd like to have on the menu? 您对菜单是否有什么特殊要求?

⑮ When would you like your banquet? 请问您想什么时候设宴?

⑯ May I know what the banquet is for? 请问这个宴会是什么类型的?

⑰ I'd like my banquet at 4,000 yuan a table excluding (or including) drinks. 我希望宴会标准是每桌4000元,不包括(或包括)饮料。

⑱ Are you in the mood for Japanese, Chinese, or some other cuisine? 您喜欢日式、中式还是其他方式的烹饪法?

⑲ I haven't decided yet. What would you suggest? 我还未决定,您有什么建议?

⑳ Chinese cooking is colorful, varied, and nutritious. 中华饮食色彩丰富,种类繁多,且注重营养。

实践实训项目
Practical Training Project

I. Building Up Your Vocabulary

1. Match the words on the left with the best translations on the right.

(1) beverage	a. 有营养的
(2) courtesy	b. 菜肴
(3) forum	c. 蛋白质
(4) banquet	d. 传统的
(5) nutritious	e. 饮品
(6) hospitality	f. 宴会
(7) protein	g. 论坛
(8) vegetarian	h. 礼貌
(9) traditional	i. 素食的
(10) cuisine	j. 热情好客

2. Complete the following dialogue with proper words or expressions.

A: I told you two days ago that we'd like to use _____(主厅) on Friday evening.

B: Well! At what time the _____(宴会) will be held?

A: The dinner party starts at 7: 00.

B: Could you please give us your menu options?

A: We'd like the _____(常规菜) and the chef's choice for the dinner party.

B: How would you like the dinner party to be served?

A: _____(法式服务). Can your crew preset the furniture for the banquet before 7: 30?

B: Sure. Our _____(客房男服务员) will take care of it.

A: What is the _____(最低消费) for each attendee?

B: Three hundred yuan per person,_____(优质品牌) excluded.

A: How are call brands charged?

B: Usually by the bottle, but we can also charge by the drink if it pleases you.

A: _____(我更喜欢前者). Is there any_____(服务费) for it?

B: Yes. There will also be other charges, such as corkage if drinks are brought from outside.

A: Well, in this case, house brands would be fine.

B: I think that can be arranged, sir. Now we haven't discussed table_____(装饰) yet.

A: I think that it would be appropriate to have the flags of the _____(参与国) on the table and some flowers.

B: What kind of flowers will there be?

A: Perhaps pink carnations would be a _____(中和色).

B: Will you be requiring any _____(背景音乐) at all?

A: I guess not. Tastes differ, you know.

B: I see. Well, we have covered all the points, haven't we?

A: Yes. By the way, put the charges on to the _____(主账).

B: Fine. If you have more requirements, _____(随时与我们联系).

A: Sure, thanks for your_____(关照).

B: _____(我们期待为您服务).

A: OK, bye!

II. Substitution Drills

Replace the underlined words with the words in the following boxes.

1. In many hotels, the banquet reservation <u>clerk</u> belongs to the Food and Beverage Department.

> staff   employee   secretary

2. For a large-scale or an important banquet reservation, however, a face-to-face talk is <u>suggested</u>.

> recommended   advised   advocated

3. When a guest comes to make the reservation in person, he will be able to give <u>detailed</u> instructions with regards to the set-up of the banquet venue, table set-up, food and beverage standard, etc.

> specific   elaborated   particular   complicated

4. It is suggested a contract be <u>concluded</u> following the negotiation.

> drawn   ended   signed up

5. Food-and-beverage functions should support the <u>objectives</u> of the meeting.

> aims   purposes   goals

6. If a corporation plans a three-day training meeting, it wants attendees to be <u>alert</u> and comfortable.

> vigilant   precautious   alarming

7. This requires balanced, nutritious, and <u>appealing</u> menus.

> attractive   absorbing   agreeable   pleasing

8. An association holding a <u>gala</u> awards dinner may have somewhat different objectives.

> festival   holiday   celebration

9. For the gala, the food must be memorable and spectacular, and the <u>atmosphere</u> must be festive.

> air   ambiance   mood

10. You will be working closely with the catering manager, who will help you plan what food and beverages will be served, the <u>type</u> of service, seating arrangements, and the decor.

> style   kind   description   model

III. Listening Comprehension

Listen to the dialogue and fill in the blanks according to what you hear. Then practice the dialogue with your partner.

W=waiter; G=guest

W: Would you like to_____ now, sir?

G: Well, what would you _____?

W: Today's special is very good. Roasted steak with _____.

G: OK, I'll take it, and a _____ , please.

W: How would you like your steak done, sir? Rare, medium, or _____ ?

G: Medium, please.

W: That's fine. How about some_____ ?

G: I just want some coffee.

W: Anything else, sir?

G: I think that is_____ for now.

W: So a vegetable soup. For the main course, medium roasted steak with fried potatoes. And some coffee.

G: Yes, that's right. Thank you.

W: You are welcome. I'll be back_____ .

IV. Role Play

Work in pairs or more. Try to act out the following situation.

Suppose you are discussing with your catering manager to work out a fancy Chinese menu for a special event. How can you make your dinner tasty and elegant?

V. Writing and Speaking

Write one sentence on your own for each of the following words or expressions and speak them out to your partner. Then your partner interprets them into Chinese.

1. banquet dinner

2. premium brands

3. service charge

4. catering service

5. dining room

6. drink list

会展之窗
The Window of the Convention & Exhibition

10 Tips for Catering Your Office Meetings & Lunches

Food, glorious food! No matter how cool we play it on the outside, it's a rare office worker who doesn't perk up at the sight of free cookies. But not all office food is created equal. Good catering can be the shining spot in a long, challenging day of meetings or training — refreshing and reviving everyone for the afternoon ahead. Bad catering can cause a million problems: slow, sluggish brains; indigestion; blood sugar crashes; and worse. If you're an office manager, it can be a lot of pressure to make sure the office lunch is a success and that your colleagues are happy!

Here's our checklist of our favorite office lunch catering ideas, tips, and tricks to help you provide the best catering for your workplace.

Get a final headcount: There's nothing like running out of food to start off a chorus of rumbling stomachs and grumbling participants. It sounds obvious, but things can change quickly and you don't want to find out five minutes before the meeting that the entire accounting team is coming and you're short of a dozen burritos.

When asking for input, be specific: If you are ordering from a takeout restaurant, a general "What would you like to eat?" can start an avalanche of opinions that will take all day to deal with. Narrow down options beforehand, provide a few clear choices, and send an email asking everyone to reply by a specified time.

Consider location: Sometimes people are expected to eat lunch in the meeting, and you'll need to set up a table in the conference room. A couple of things to keep in mind: place the table opposite from the presentation area so that participants can go back for a refill without crossing in front, and avoid messy or noisy foods. Trying to crunch a taco silently while watching a PowerPoint presentation is a cruel and unusual torture.

Think about time: If there's an especially packed schedule and people only have a short time to eat, setup can be everything. This is when all eyes are on the office admin! Individually packed paper bag lunches prevent long, frustrating lines to get to food; control portions; and also give folks the freedom of a "to go" option if they need to get right back into the meeting room.

Don't forget the extras: Napkins, hand sanitizers, wet wipes, mints, and other thoughtful touches can help everything run a bit more neatly and easily.

Go seasonal: If there's a holiday around the corner, think about adding a few hints to the decor and food. It doesn't need to be a full-on office party to inject a little fun into the proceedings. However, if there is an upcoming holiday such as Mardi Gras or Cinco de Mayo, use it as a theme to choose the food and decor for your office gathering. Use your imagination and brighten up everyone's day.

Offer some agency: Giving people a little power over what they eat can be refreshing for a captive audience. It can also save the office organizer from taking 20 individual sandwich orders. Instead, buy the components for a salad and sandwich bar and let everyone customize their own. Keep things neat, convenient, and authentic with real deli accessories.

Think about food sensitivities: I know, if you hear about Paleo one more time... but the fact is, planning ahead can cut down on whining and make you a champion to the resident CrossFitters. It's impossible to keep everyone happy all the time, but these days having a gluten-free option and a vegan option is a good start. In fact, it's practically essential.

Make the healthy options fun: Be honest, how many apples have you thrown away? Almost everyone bypasses the fruit bowl for the candy jar, but you still need to make an effort to provide wholesome food. Try offering something like an Edible Arrangement and healthier but still enticing snack options like Sun Chips or Luna Bars.

Satisfy the sweet tooth: As long as you've got some healthy options, don't skimp on the occasional treat. Sometimes the thought of that delicious cupcake or pastry is the only thing keeping us going.

As office manager, you've got a lot on your plate, and being in charge of getting everyone fed and watered on a budget can be demanding. But the way to a workforce's heart is through its stomach, so get it right and your coworkers will love you for it!

Unit Eight

会后观光

Post-conference Travel

Teaching Targets 教学目标

- To learn about the importance of post-conference tour
- To get a general idea of post-conference tour
- To master some useful professional words, phrases, and key sentence patterns
- To hold conversations concerning this topic

背景知识
Background Knowledge

　　会后旅游是会展旅游的一种，广义上也属于商务旅游范畴，一般指会议接待者利用召开会议的机会，组织与会者参加的旅游活动。会后旅游往往带有与工作相关的目的。

　　事实上，会议活动和休闲旅游活动是经常交织在一起的。在繁忙、紧张的会议之后，抽出一定时间为参会嘉宾安排一些休闲旅游活动，不失为一项明智之举。这些活动不仅能够舒缓他们繁重的工作和生活压力，消除身心疲劳，还能够给他们带来极大的精神激励、满足感、成就感和荣誉感。

热身活动
Warming Up

Listen to the recording carefully and answer the following questions.

　　1. What is integrated with meetings as a common practice?

　　2. What is the purpose of incentive travel?

　　3. How do you incorporate meetings and incentive travel?

示范对话
Model Dialogues

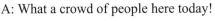
Dialogue 1

(At an art show, Berry is showing an art show to a tourist.)

A=a tourist; B=Berry

A: What a crowd of people here today!

B: It is nothing unusual. For it's a joint art show of world famous artists, both past and present.

A: So that's why there are so many foreigners among the crowd.

B: Let's go in.

A: What's this?

B: It's "Guernica". It's made by Picasso in 1937, aiming at commemorating a town bombed by German planes. Look here, it looks somewhat like a dying horse, and this is said to be murdered children. So it's a picture of a ruined world with strange shapes of dying horse and murdered children.

A: No wonder it looks so terrible.

B: Your feeling shows you are quite outstanding. For it's a really violent expression of revolt against the horror of modern warfare.

A: Thank you for your flattering words. Is this, "The Blue Rider", a watercolor?

B: Yes. It was produced by Kandinsky in about 1910. Perhaps it was the first example of a form of abstract expressionism.

A: I know this one. It's a traditional Chinese painting.

B: You're right. And this "Plum and Bamboo" was one of Zhen Banqiao's masterpieces.

A: And this is Qi Baishi's "Chickens and Stone".

B: Yes. This long scroll is a Gongbi.

A: What does Gongbi mean?

B: Gongbi is a traditional Chinese realistic painting characterized by fine brushwork and close attention to details.

A: Oh, look. So many kangaroos. Is this some kind of watercolor?

B: Something like that, but not exactly the same. It's called gouache.

A: Oh, it's 11: 30 already. Let's go for lunch and we'll then go on with our business.

B: OK.

Word bank

joint [dʒɔɪnt] *adj.* 共同的；连接的；联合的 *v.* 连接，贴合

commemorate [kə'meməreɪt] *v.* 庆祝；纪念；成为……的纪念

violent ['vaɪəl(ə)nt] *adj.* 暴力的；猛烈的

revolt [rɪ'vəʊlt] *n.* 反抗；叛乱 *v.* 反抗；反叛

flatter ['flætə] *v.* 奉承；谄媚；使高兴

abstract ['æbstrækt] *adj.* 抽象的；深奥的 *n.* 摘要；抽象

masterpiece ['mɑːstəpiːs] *n.* 杰作；绝无仅有的人

characterize ['kærəktə'raɪz] *v.* 以……为特性；具有……的特征

gouache [guː'ɑːʃ; gwɑːʃ] *n.* 水粉画；树胶水彩画；水粉颜料

Notes

1. For it's a joint art show of world famous artists, both past and present.

   因为这里在举办世界著名的古今艺术家的联合画展。

2. It's made by Picasso in 1937, aiming at commemorating a town bombed by German planes.

   这是毕加索1937年创作的，旨在纪念被德国飞机炸毁的一个小镇。

3. For it's a really violent expression of revolt against the horror of modern warfare.

   因为这幅画正是反抗现代战争之恐怖的一种强烈的表达。

4. Perhaps it was the first example of a form of abstract expressionism.

   可能它是抽象表现主义的第一个代表作。

5. Gongbi is a traditional Chinese realistic painting characterized by fine brushwork and close attention to details.

   工笔是中国传统的写实主义画法，以用笔细腻和注重细节为特征。

Dialogue 2

(Walking along Hanzheng Street, Berry and her tour group are talking about this famous shopping center.)

A=Berry; B=tour members

A: Here we are. We are now in Hanzheng Street.

B: There are so many people here and there. We are really in a big shopping center.

A: Exactly. Hanzheng Street is indeed the most popular place for shopping and sightseeing.

B: I enjoy wandering from one place to another.

A: It would be regretful to have been to Wuhan without having a tour around Hanzheng Street. Hanzheng Street is so named because it was once the main street of Hankou. With a history of more than 500 years, it is one of the oldest streets in Wuhan. In the late Qing Dynasty and the early Republic of China, merchants and traders flocked around the area and markets thrived along the street, assuming a prosperous scene.

B: A street with 500 years of history. But now it has a new look with so many modern high buildings.

A: Yes. Things are changing with the passage of time. Hanzheng Street having experienced many rises and falls, has grown into the biggest collecting and distributing center for small commodities in central China.

B: By the way, how long is the street?

A: The principal street is more than 1,600 meters in length. It faces the Han River and extends alongside the east bank of the Changjiang River. Connecting 117 lanes on its sides, it has an area of about 2.56 square km.

B: Where can we see the old buildings with 500 years of history?

A: Along the Big and Small Qianlong Lanes of Hanzheng Street, buildings of the Qing Dynasty are well preserved.

B: Shall we go there and have a look?

A: OK. And the scheme of developing the street of Ancient Buildings has been included into the city plans.

B: Are the goods cheaper here than those in the big department stores?

A: Yes. With its cheap commodity prices, a complete variety of goods, and peculiar humanistic landscape, this street attracts a large number of businessmen, customers, and tourists every day.

B: Where can I buy some souvenirs?

A: Along the lane for handicrafts, gifts, and souvenirs, you will find toys, handicrafts, pot plants, and flowers. They are numerous in variety and pleasing to one's eyes.

B: Let's go there later.

Word bank

sightseeing ['saɪtsiɪŋ] *n.* 观光；游览

wander ['wɒndə] *v.* 徘徊；漫步

flock [flɒk] *v.* 聚集；成群而行 *n.* 群

thrive [θraɪv] *v.* 繁荣，兴旺；茁壮成长

assume [ə'sjuːm] *v.* 呈现；假定；承担

prosperous ['prɒsp(ə)rəs] *adj.* 繁荣的；兴旺的

distribute [dɪ'strɪbjut] *v.* 分配；散布；分开

commodity [kə'mɒdɪtɪ] *n.* 商品；货物；日用品

Notes

1. Hanzheng Street is indeed the most popular place for shopping and sightseeing.

汉正街确实是最受欢迎的购物和观光之地。

2. I enjoy wandering from one place to another.

我喜欢一处接一处地漫游。

3. In the late Qing Dynasty and the early Republic of China, merchants and traders flocked around the area and markets thrive along the street, assuming a prosperous scene.

在晚清时期和民国初期，商人和贸易者们聚集于此地，街旁商铺林立，一片繁荣景象。

4. Things are changing with the passage of time. Hanzheng Street having experienced many rises and falls, has grown into the biggest collecting and distributing center for small commodities in central China.

事物总是随着时间在改变，汉正街经历了很多起伏，已经发展为中国中部地区的小商品集散中心。

5. Along the Big and Small Qianlong Lanes of Hanzheng Street, buildings of the Qing Dynasty are well preserved.

沿着汉正街大大小小的"乾隆巷"，清代的建筑在那里保存完好。

6. With its cheap commodity prices, a complete variety of goods, and peculiar humanistic landscape, this street attracts a large number of businessmen, customers, and tourists every day.

这条街以其便宜的物价、齐全的货品和独特的人文景观每天都吸引着大批的商人、消费者和游客。

实用句型
Practical Sentence Patterns

1 You look so beautiful tonight. 今晚您看上去真美啊!

2 I've really had a good time tonight. 今晚我过得很开心。

3 Excuse me. Could you tell me where the tourist information center is? 打扰一下，您能告诉我旅游咨询处在哪儿吗?

4 I'm new here. You had better ask the policeman over there. 我初来此地，您最好问问那边的警察。

⑤ Can you recommend a hotel which is not too expensive? 您能推荐一家较为廉价的旅馆吗？

⑥ I'd like to stay at a hotel near the beach. 我想要住在一间靠近海滩的旅馆。

⑦ There is a Moonlight Hotel with excellent service near the beach. 有个月光宾馆，离海滩不远，而且服务是一流的。

⑧ Please tell me about some interesting places in this city. 请告诉我这座城市里一些有趣的地方。

⑨ I want to visit some historic sites. 我想参观一些历史名胜。

⑩ What are the places of special interest here? 这里有什么特别有趣的地方吗？

⑪ Why don't you go to the Disneyland? I'm sure you'll have fun there. 何不去迪士尼乐园玩玩呢？我相信您在那儿肯定会玩得很开心。

⑫ Do you have a sightseeing brochure for the city? 您有这座城市的旅游手册吗？

⑬ I'd like to know the route of the streetcar. 我想知道电车行进的路线。

⑭ How much dose it cost if I stay there for two weeks? 我如果在那儿待两周，要多少钱？

⑮ How about going to the Oriental Pearl TV Tower first? 先去东方明珠电视塔如何？

⑯ We are arranging a sightseeing schedule for you. 我们正在为您安排观光的计划。

实践实训项目
Practical Training Project

I. Building Up Your Vocabulary

1. Match the words on the left with the best translations on the right.

(1) tourist   a. 纪念品

(2) sightseeing   b. 风景

(3) commodity   c. 漫步

(4) flatter   d. 繁荣的

(5) commemorate   e. 商品

(6) souvenir   f. 夸赞

(7) landscape   g. 代表作

(8) wander   h. 观光

(9) prosperous   i. 纪念

(10) masterpiece   j. 游客

2. Complete the following sentences with proper words or expressions.

(1) Welcome to Hubei province. I'm Berry, your _____(导游) for this tour.

(2) Wuhan is the capital of Hubei Province. It is _____(政治、经济、金融和文化中心) of the province.

(3) There are _____(超出) 7 million people living here.

(4) Let me introduce _____(道教) to you first.

(5) I have visited many temples in China, but I had thought they were all _____(佛教的) temples.

(6) They are_____ (单元式住宅) for city residents.

(7) We are going to cross the _____(长江大桥).

(8) For quite a long time before 1957, ferry was the only _____(现代化手段) of transport for people to cross the river.

(9) It was slow in speed and, what's more, it would have to stop working whenever there were _____(大浪) or big flood.

(10) It is the first combined bridge over the Changjiang River. Its main bridge is 1,156 meters in length, its deck is 22.5 meters in width, and the _____(最大跨径) section is 128 meters in length.

II. Substitution Drills

Replace the underlined words with the words in the following boxes.

1. Today, in order to motivate employees to invest extra efforts in work, they must be offered something more than a <u>pleasant</u> experience.

| glad | happy | favorable |

2. It is not only a trip any more, but an experience on the trip which would enliven them with surprises, special moments, and <u>unusual</u> events — the experience they can not relive... no matter how rich they are.

| uncommon | different | distinctive |

3. The incentive travel basically implies <u>unforgettable</u> and entertaining trips paid by employers, with the main purpose of encouraging employees to reach challenging business goals of the company by achieving individual and/or group goals.

| memorable | indelible | impressive |

4. The incentive travel is <u>predominantly</u> used with the basic aim of increasing sales.

| primarily | mainly | mostly | largely | basically |

5. Incentive travel is a global management tool that uses an exceptional travel experience

to <u>motivate</u> and/or recognize participants for increased levels of performance in support of organizational goals.

> activate   stimulate   encourage

6. In some developing markets (such as the Indian market), the incentive travel <u>implies</u> a simple arrangement or only a plane ticket and paid accommodation.

> means   refers to   involves

7. In the USA for instance, there is a <u>considerable</u> number of individual incentives using catalogue offer as incentive programmes.

> large   great   many

8. However, the majority of traditional incentive trips imply a group of people for whom an activity and entertainment programme is <u>tailored</u>.

> customized   made-to-order   formulated

9. Industries mostly using incentive trips are those operating in <u>extremely</u> competitive sectors where retaining or increasing market shares demands constant great efforts in the sale and management fields, making them incentive trip consumers in their nature.

> highly   greatly   exceedingly

10. <u>Generally</u>, the largest buyers of incentive programmes come from the automotive industry, financial services, office equipment industry, electronics, telecommunications, and tobacco industry, etc.

> by and large   as a rule   in general   broadly speaking

III. Listening Comprehension

Listen to the dialogue and fill in the blanks according to what you hear. Then practice the dialogue with your partner.

A=tour guide; B= Black

A: Excuse me. You're Black from _____, aren't you?

B: Yes. I'm glad you_____ me.

A: Let me introduce myself: I'm Berry, the _____from Beijing. How do you do?

B: How do you do? I'm glad to know you. Pardon me. I didn't quite _____ your name just now. Would you please_____ it?

A: It's Berry.

B: May I know your Chinese name?

A: Certainly. It's Li Ping. Li is my _____, but the Chinese put the surname first.

B: Li Ping. Am I right?

A: Quite right. Do you have any unaccompanied_____?

B: No. I always travel with these two bags.

A: Let's go, then. This way to the front-door. Let me _____ your bags.

B: No, I wouldn't _____of letting a lady carry things for me. Surely I'm not so old as all that yet.

A: Of course not. You look young and energetic in spite of your_____hair.

B: Thank you. I'm glad to hear that.

A: The car is waiting outside to take us to the hotel. I've reserved a _____ for you at Good Luck Hotel, one of the biggest in Beijing.

B: Do you mean one of the_____suites, or one of the biggest hotels?

A: Actually, both the hotel and suite are _____big.

B: That will be nice.

IV. Role Play

Work in pairs or more. Try to act out the following situations.

1. Suppose you are a tour guide/tour leader. You need to receive a tour group at the assembling place.

Tour guide: Li Ping. Tour leader: Black.

Tour group: Good Luck Tour Group from Beijing, 20 members.

Arrival time: 8 a.m.

2. Suppose you are Miss Li, the operator of a travel agency. You are confirming the itinerary with Black, the client, and you have to make some adjustment on the itinerary.

V. Writing and Speaking

Write one sentence on your own for each of the following words or expressions and speak them out to your partner. Then your partner interprets them into Chinese.

1. tourist information center

2. excellent service

3. interesting places

4. historic sites

5. the Disneyland

6. sightseeing brochure

会展之窗
The Window of the Convention & Exhibition

Incentive Travel

1. A Unique Approach for Improving the Effectiveness of Meetings and Incentive Travel

A unique process is a comprehensive, people-driven approach that includes a proven research component. The full target population for the meeting or incentive travel reward is invited to participate in the survey. Respondents are presented with a wide range of program elements in different combinations and are asked to weigh their importance. Meeting and incentive travel elements such as trip length, time of year, destination, guest policy, general session speakers, meeting format, activities, etc. are evaluated. The results of the survey give senior management and meeting planners real data to back up program enhancements or deletions. Attendees experience the changes and feel they have co-created the program. One client used this approach to develop an event measurement scorecard. It measured pre-event and post-event scores against participants' understanding, belief, or commitment to corporate goals and messages. By comparing the pre-event and post-event researches, the client was able to see the marketing message absorption after the trip remained neutral to negative. This provided the event team the opportunity to create a communications plan beyond the event to improve the message absorption. Had they not run the pre-event and post-event researches, this need would have gone unmeasured.

2. Where Successful Incentive Tours and Travel Programs Begin

If you want to take your meetings and incentive travel programs to the next level, turn to the professional team in incentive tours. With their experience and expertise, they can help you provide unforgettable experiences for your participants, planners, and stakeholders. With their unique approach, they can help you improve the effectiveness of your meetings and incentive travel rewards. And ultimately, they will help you develop a meeting and incentive travel strategy that drives business results. Are you ready for logistical expertise, more effective outcomes, and strategic alignment of your meeting and incentive travel strategies? Then it's time to contact the incentive travel experts.

Article Source:

http://www.cra-arc.gc.ca/visitors/

Part

Two

展览英语

English for Exhibitions

Unit Nine

展会特性确认

Confirming the Characters of the Exhibition

Teaching Targets 教学目标

- To learn about what comprehensive exhibition & professional exhibition are
- To learn about the characters of an exhibition
- To master some useful expressions and sentences
- To hold conversations concerning this topic

背景知识
Background Knowledge

展览会通常有以下分类方式。

1. 按展览性质划分

展览会按展览性质分为贸易展和消费展两种。

贸易展是为制造业、商业等行业举办的展览。展览的主要目的是交流信息、洽谈贸易。

消费展是为公众举办的展览，基本上展出消费品，目的是直接销售。

展览的性质由展览组织者决定，可以通过参观者的组成反映出来：对工商界开放的展览会是贸易展，对公众开放的展览会是消费展。

2. 按展览内容划分

展览会按展览内容分为综合展览和专业展览两种。

综合展览指包括全行业或数个行业的展览会，也被称为横向型展览会，如工业展、轻工业展。

专业展览指展示某一行业甚至某一项产品的展览会，如钟表展。专业展览的突出特征是常常同时举办讨论会、报告会，以介绍新产品、新技术。

3. 按展览规模划分

展览会按展览规模分为国际展、国家展、地区展、地方展，以及单个公司的独家展。规模是指展出者和参观者所代表的区域规模，而不是展览场地规模。不同规模的展览会有不同的特色和优势，企业应根据自身条件和需要来选择。

4. 按展览时间划分

展览会按展览时间分为定期和不定期两种。

定期展会有一年四次、一年两次、一年一次、两年一次等。不定期展会视需要和条件举办，分长期展和短期展。长期展可以是三个月展、半年展，甚至常设展，短期展的时间间隔一般不超过一个月。在发达国家/地区，专业贸易展览会一般持续三天。

热身活动
Warming Up

Listen to the recording carefully and answer the following questions.

1. What is an exhibition according to this passage?

2. What are the types of exhibitions?

3. What's the purpose of holding museums?

4. Can art exhibitions be commercial?

5. What are the differences between trade shows and consumer exhibitions?

示范对话
Model Dialogues

Dialogue 1

A is introducing exhibitions to the customers (i.e. B).

A: Good morning. This is Guangzhou International Exhibition Group. Can I help you?

B: Yes, we'd like to know more about the International Food & Beverage Exhibition in September. Is there any free space?

A: Please wait a moment. Let me check... Yes, how big of the place would you prefer?

B: We have no idea whether we will take part in or not, because we are a manufacturer of the food-processing machines.

A: This is a comprehensive exhibition, which includes raw materials, products, machines, and some media stuff. It's an overall and wide-ranging exhibition.

B: But we don't know how many enterprises in our industry will take part in.

A: We have data from the past years. Machine manufacturers accounted for 29% of this exhibition, and based on this type of professional exhibition, most of the buyers prefer to the one-stop purchasing.

B: Sounds great. Please send me last year's proportion, and we will consider about it carefully.

Word bank

beverage ['bev(ə)rɪdʒ] *n.* 饮料
manufacturer [ˌmænju'fæktʃərə] *n.* 制造商；[经] 厂商
comprehensive [kɒmprɪ'hensɪv] *adj.* 综合的；广泛的；有理解力的

raw [rɔː] *adj.* 生的；未加工的；阴冷的；刺痛的；擦掉皮的；无经验的

overall [ˈəʊvərɔːl] *adj.* 全部的；全体的；一切在内的

enterprise [ˈentəpraɪz] *n.* 企业；事业；进取心；事业心

account [əˈkaʊnt] *v.* 认为；把...视为 *n.* 账户；解释；账目，账单；理由

proportion [prəˈpɔːʃ(ə)n] *n.* 比例；部分；面积

Notes

1. We'd like to know more about the International Food & Beverage Exhibition in September. Is there any free space?

我们想要了解下9月份的国际食品饮品展，还有空余的位置吗？

2. We have no idea whether we will take part in or not, because we are a manufacturer of the food-making machine.

我不知道我们是否会参加，因为我们是食品机械制造商。

3. This is a comprehensive exhibition, which includes raw materials, products, machine, and some media stuff.

这是一个综合性展会，包括原材料、产品、机械和一些媒介材料。

4. We have data from the past years. Machine manufacturers accounted for 29% of this exhibition, and based on this type of professional exhibition, most of the buyers prefer to the one-stop purchasing.

往年的数据显示，29%的参展企业为机械制造商。而且基于这类专业展会，大多数买家喜好一站式采购。

5. Please send me last year's proportion, and we will consider about it carefully.

请把去年的参展商比例情况发给我，我们会认真地考虑。

Dialogue 2

A is helping the exhibitors (i.e. B) to choose a suitable exhibition.

A: Good morning. This is Guangzhou International Exhibition Group. What can I do for you?

B: We'd like to know which types of exhibitions we could take part in? We can supply raw materials for beverages.

A: Please wait a moment. Let me check the database. There is an International Food & Beverage Raw Material Exhibition on September 8th and an Organic Beverage Raw Material

Exhibition on September 28th. They are very close and you can get more information about them.

B: What's the difference between these two exhibitions?

A: They are both for the raw materials, but I think the International Food & Beverage Raw Material Exhibition is better than the other one.

B: But our product is more professional with less clients — it's not very common for visitors.

A: Ah, according to your description, I suggest you take part in the International Food & Beverage Raw Material Exhibition. I will send you the instructions about the two exhibitions. You can compare them and make your decision.

B: That's great. Thanks a lot.

Word bank

suitable ['suːtəb(ə)l] *adj.* 适当的；相配的
supply [sə'plaɪ] *n.* 供给，补给；供应品 *v.* 供给，提供
material [mə'tɪərɪəl] *n.* 材料；原料；物资
database ['deɪtəbeɪs] *n.* 数据库，资料库
organic [ɔː'gænɪk] *adj.* 有机的；组织的；器官的
description [dɪ'skrɪpʃ(ə)n] *n.* 描述，描写；类型；说明书
instruction [ɪn'strʌkʃ(ə)n] *n.* 指令，命令；指示
compare [kəm'peə] *v.* 比较；比拟；喻为

Notes

1. We'd like to know which types of exhibitions we could take part in? We can supply raw materials for beverages.

我们想知道我们可以参加哪种类型的展会？我们能够供应制作饮料的原料。

2. Please wait a moment. Let me check the database.

请稍等。我查一下数据库。

3. What's the difference between these two exhibitions?

两个展会有什么区别吗？

4. They are both for the raw materials, but I think the International Food & Beverage Raw Material Exhibition is better than the other one.

它们都面向原材料市场，但是我认为国际食品饮品原材料展比另一个要好些。

5. I will send you the instructions about the two exhibitions. You can compare them and make your decision.

我会给您寄送两个展会的说明，您可以比较一下，然后做出决定。

实用句型
Practical Sentence Patterns

1 We'd like to get some information about the International Food & Beverage Exhibition in September. 我们想了解一下9月份的国际食品饮品展。

2 This is an all-round and large-scale exhibition. 这是个综合性强、规模宏大的展会。

3 But we don't know how many enterprises in our industry will participate in. 但是我们不知道我们行业内有多少企业会参展。

4 Please send me the proportion of the past years, and we will consider about it. 请把往年的参展商比例情况发给我，我们考虑一下。

5 This exhibition will be more suitable for your company. 这次展会将很适合贵公司。

6 We'd like to know which kind of exhibitions in October we could participate in. We can supply raw materials of food. 我们想了解一下10月份有哪些展会可以参加。我们是提供食品原料的。

7 What's the difference between these two exhibitions? 这两个展会有什么不同？

8 According to your description, I suggest you take part in the International Food Raw Material Exhibition. 根据您的描述，我建议您参加国际食品原料博览会。

9 We can supply water-purifying equipment. Is there any similar company in this exhibition? 我们是提供净水设备的，这个展会中有类似的公司吗？

10 We mainly manufacture equipment for industry. 我们主要生产工业设备。

11 The main purpose of this Eastern Asia Water Treatment Exhibition is to show and market the home water-purifying equipment, and it is very professional. 此次东亚水处理展的主要目标是对家用净水设备进行展示和推广，专业性很强。

12 The participants promoting the industry water-purifying equipment are not so many as the home ones. 工业净水设备的参展商没有家用净水设备的多。

13 Most of the participants of this exhibition are small agents. 参展的主要是一些小型的代理商。

14 We think the Global Water Treatment Exhibition in April will be more suitable for

your products. 我们认为 4 月份的环球水处理展更适合您的产品。

⑮ In that exhibition, most of the visitors are tenderers from the government and purchasers of engineering projects. 那个展会的访客主要是一些政府投标人员和工程项目采购人员。

⑯ I will send you the data about this exhibition. 我将把该展会的相关资料发送给您。

实践实训项目
Practical Training Project

I. Building Up Your Vocabulary

1. Match the words on the left with the best translations on the right.

(1) manufacturer   a. 描述

(2) enterprise   b. 采购商

(3) large-scale   c. 比较

(4) consumer   d. 供应

(5) commercial   e. 比例

(6) purchaser   f. 制造商

(7) proportion   g. 商业的

(8) compare   h. 大规模的

(9) description   i. 企业

(10) supply   j. 消费者

2. Complete the following dialogue with proper words or expressions.

A: Hello, is that Guangzhou International Exhibition Group? I learn from the_____(官网) that you are the organizer of the International Exhibition of Equipment and Technologies for Water Treatment.

B: Yes, how may I assist you?

A: We can supply softened water treatment equipment. Is there any _____(相似的公司) in this exhibition?

B: Is the softened water treatment equipment made for industry or family?

A: We _____(主要生产) equipment for industry.

B: _____(主要目的) of this exhibition is to show and market the water treatment equipment for home, and it is _____(非常专业). The participants promoting the industry softened water equipment are not so many as the home ones. Most of the participants of this exhibition are small agents, so we think the China Water Expo in June will be _____(更适合您们的产品). In that exhibition, most of the visitors are tenderers from the government and _____(采购商) of engineering projects, so it seems more appropriate for you, and I will send you the information about this exhibition.

A: Oh, got it. Thank you very much.

B: You are welcome.

II. Substitution Drills

Replace the underlined words with the words in the following boxes.

1. Trade shows began as small company meetings that grew into industry events which showcased companies and their products and services.

displayed   exhibited   showed   presented

2. The exchange of information is a priceless interaction between the attendees and exhibitors.

valuable   precious   worthy

3. Depending on the industry and size of the trade show, the exhibition will run anywhere from three to five days or more and usually take place in large cities and metropolitan areas.

scale   scope   dimension

4. Attendees are drawn to special features such as keynote speakers, special guests, and promotions for free products and services.

characteristics   marks   qualities

5. The most popular trade shows are those in the technology and consumer electronics industries.

pop   prevailing   common

6. Attendees also make networking contacts for marketing, advertising, and employment.

communication   exchanges   links   interactions

7. The major benefit for these companies is that new products are introduced to eager businesses and consumers, several months or years before they are available commercially.

interested   enthusiastic   willing

8. Exhibitors make sure their products are in top form functionally, to make a strong first

impression and create a <u>buzz</u> within the industry.

| excitement   inspiration   stimulation |

9. Another popular <u>example</u> is trade shows and exhibitions in the arts and entertainment industry.

| instance   case   illustration |

10. This is an <u>integral</u> aspect of business growth for the entrepreneur because it involves having several people from one industry in a single setting, discussing issues pertinent to the business.

| indispensable   necessary   essential |

III. Listening Comprehension

Listen to the dialogue and fill in the blanks according to what you hear. Then practice the dialogue with your partner.

A: This is Guangzhou International Exhibition Group. May I help you?

B: Is this the place for the International _____ in September?

Are there any exhibition booths _____?

A: What's your _____?

B: We are motor parts manufacturers.

A: Oh, the distribution of this exhibition is according to the composition of different _____, and here is a special area for the motor parts manufacturers and it is almost like a small _____ exhibition, which may be better than other professional ones. For this industry, many detail parts have been divided, so this exhibition will be more _____ for your company.

B: Really? Can you show me the _____ from last year?

A: No problem.

IV. Role Play

Work in pairs or more. Try to act out the following situation.

Suppose you are working for a water treatment equipment trading company which is going to participate in an exhibition abroad. You are negotiating with a manager of the exhibition company about the participating fee.

V. Writing and Speaking

Write one sentence on your own for each of the following words or expressions and speak them out to your partner. Then your partner interprets them into Chinese.

1. Food & Beverage

2. all-round

3. large-scale

4. raw materials

5. manufacture equipment

6. main purpose

7. small agents

8. more suitable

会展之窗
The Window of the Convention & Exhibition

The Future Role of Exhibitions in the Marketing Mix

Commerce is in our blood. We love to buy and sell, and we love to meet people. It is no wonder then that trade shows and exhibitions have always been an important marketing tool. In fact, from a historical perspective, they probably can be seen as the "mother" of marketing. But just like anything else in this world, exhibitions have been undergoing a constant transformation ever since.

Is Digital the Future of Marketing?

As a unique promotion tool, trade shows hold a special place in the marketing mix. They unite individuals on a show floor and allow vendors to speak to potential clients face-to-face. In addition to that, they provide an intense experience on a multi-sensual level. However, with the digitalization of marketing, trade shows are recently experiencing one of the biggest transformations in their existence. The mere participation in a show might not deliver the marketing value that it did just 10–15 years ago.

CEIR recently found that 98% of young exhibitors see a unique value in trade shows that cannot be fulfilled by other marketing channels, so apparently the young generation of marketers appreciate the potential and the unique value of exhibitions. At the same time, however, we know how demanding "Generation Y" are and how tech-savvy they are. It is vital to listen to them, hear what their expectations are, and find out how the exhibition industry can respond to their needs.

Technology and Shows, a Hell of a Marketing Couple

There is huge marketing potential in technology usage and digital engagement at trade shows. It becomes easier than ever to reach masses of people through the devices that show visitors' use. There are tons of possibilities to get targeted messages to potential clients, communicate specific product information to them, and simply generate buzz from a company's trade show participation.

Thanks to the apps, on-site engagement tools, and NFC technologies like iBeacons, communication goes well beyond the "basic" mass email approach as exhibitors now have the ability to push marketing messages directly to visitors passing their booth.

The challenge for exhibition organizers in order to retain clients lies in identifying and communicating clear advantages their exhibitors will get from a show. Successful exhibitions usually connect the show environment with the "digital world" and are visible to their clients 365 days a year — through social media and valuable content. To think out of the box and to extend trade shows outside the halls will be key to retaining clients and improving the event experience in the future.

Connecting the Dots

So how does this transformation of marketing and exhibitions reflect in the marketing mix? I strongly believe that the "art" of marketing is to connect the power of face-to-face with the benefits of the digitalization we are currently experiencing. Within this beautiful connection of differing elements in the marketing mix, trade shows still hold their very own, very special place, now, and in the future.

As a marketer and a trade show enthusiast, I'd love to hear your opinion on the future role of exhibitions within the marketing mix.

Unit Ten

贸易展
Trade Show

Teaching Targets 教学目标

- To learn about the basic concept of trade show
- To understand the elements of a successful trade show and the effectiveness of participating in a trade show
- To master some useful expressions and sentences
- To hold conversations concerning this topic

背景知识
Background Knowledge

贸易展是一个特定行业内的公司为展示其新产品或服务而组织和举办的展会。通常来讲，贸易展不对大众开放，只有公司代表和媒体人员能够参加。

热身活动
Warming Up

Listen to the recording carefully and answer the following questions.

1. What should you consider when deciding to exhibit your products or services?

2. What are the benefits for exhibitors to attend an exhibition?

3. What are the benefits for visitors to attend an exhibition?

示范对话
Model Dialogues

Dialogue 1

Tom (i.e. T) and Fred (i.e. F) are talking about trade shows.

T: Good morning, Fred.

F: Good morning, Tom. How is it going?

T: Not too bad. I'm reading some articles about trade shows. I'd like to ask you some questions. The first question is: What benefits can I expect if I exhibit at trade shows?

F: Well, you can use trade shows to promote your products or services.

T: Yes, but can you be more specific?

F: Of course. You may know that exhibiting at trade shows is an effective way to test new markets or launch new products and services. Trade shows offer you an opportunity to present your products or services to customers face-to-face.

T: I see.

F: Trade shows are also good opportunities for building new business, since many potential customers and suppliers are concentrated in one place.

T: Thank you for your professional opinion. I wonder what's the most important thing to know about if I want to exhibit at a trade show.

F: For an exhibitor, choosing an appropriate trade show is essential. If the trade show is too specialized or too broad, it's unlikely to attract visitors who want to buy what you sell, and participating in trade shows can be a waste of time. So you see, when you attend a trade show, you should make sure what kind of customers you want to reach and what you want to achieve.

T: Anything else I should know?

F: One more thing. You should make specific and measurable goals.

If you choose your show carefully and give yourself enough time to plan your goals, you'll have a good chance of doing successful business.

T: Great! You are a real specialist. Thanks a lot.

F: You are welcome.

Word bank

article ['ɑːtɪk(ə)l] *n.* 文章；物品

exhibit [ɪg'zɪbɪt] *v.* 展览；显示 *n.* 展览品

promote [prə'məʊt] *v.* 促进；提升；推销

specialist ['speʃ(ə)lɪst] *n.* 专家；专门医师

appropriate [ə'prəʊprɪət] *adj.* 适当的；恰当的；合适的

participate [pɑː'tɪsɪpeɪt] *v.* 参与，参加

measurable ['meʒ(ə)rəb(ə)l] *adj.* 可测量的；重要的

goal [ɡəʊl] *n.* 目标；球门

Notes

1. Well, you can use trade shows to promote your products or services.

   您能够利用贸易展推广您的产品或服务。

2. You may know that exhibiting at trade shows is an effective way to test new markets or launch new products and services.

   您可能知道参加贸易展是检测新市场和发布新产品和服务的有效方式。

3. Trade shows offer you an opportunity to present your products or services to customers face-to-face.

贸易展为您提供一个面对面向消费者展示产品或服务的机会。

4. Trade shows are also good opportunities for building new business since many potential customers and suppliers are concentrated in one place.

贸易展也是建立新业务的良好机会，因为很多潜在的客户和供应商都集中在一个地方。

5. If the trade show is too specialized or too broad, it's unlikely to attract visitors who want to buy what you sell, and participating in trade shows can be a waste of time.

如果贸易展太专业或宽泛，很可能不会吸引到那些想要购买您销售的产品的参观者，而参加贸易展可能会变成浪费时间的事。

Dialogue 2

At a trade show.

S=salesman; I=importer

S: Good morning. Can I help you?

I: I wonder if you can give me specific information about this computer model you're presenting.

S: I'd be happy to help.

I: Thank you. I see your computer is fully IBM compatible.

S : Yes, this model can run any software an IBM personal computer can run.

I : These models seem to be quite small.

S: Yes, one of the problems our company was trying to solve when we worked on this model was to do away with the bulk of IBM desk-tops and their clones. Our computer is only 11 pounds.

I: Amazing! There's nothing quite like seeing a problem and solving it to create a good product. Are all the components made in Taiwan?

S: Yes. May I ask what company you work for?

I: I represent Dell Computer and Supply Company. We're a high-volume, discount mail-order house.

S: Would you like to visit our factory?

I: Yes, if it wouldn't take too long to arrange. I'm due to fly back to our country on Tuesday.

S: I'm sure we can arrange it before then. How about meeting the CEO of our company? Would you be interested in talking with him about our ideas for upcoming models?

I : Yes, I think that would be useful. Thank you for your help.

S: You are welcome.

Word bank

compatible [kəm'pætɪb(ə)l] *adj.* 兼容的；能共处的；可并立的

bulk [bʌlk] *n.* 体积，容量；大多数，大部分；大块

clone [kləʊn] *n.* 克隆

component [kəm'pəʊnənt] *n.* 成分；组件 *adj.* 组成的，构成的

supply [sə'plaɪ] *n.* 供给，补给；供应品 *v.* 供给，提供

discount ['dɪskaʊnt] *n.* 折扣；贴现率

upcoming [ʌp'kʌmɪŋ] *adj.* 即将来临的

Notes

1. I wonder if you can give me specific information about this computer model you're presenting.

我想知道您能否提供您展示的计算机型号的具体信息。

2. I see your computer is fully IBM compatible.

我了解到您家的计算机完全兼容IBM.

3. One of the problems our company was trying to solve when we worked on this model was to do away with the bulk of IBM desk-tops and their clones.

当我们公司研制这个型号时，试图解决的问题之一就是摒弃IBM台式电脑和其他克隆电脑的大体积。

4. Amazing! There's nothing quite like seeing a problem and solving it to create a good product.

太棒了！发现并解决问题的同时创造出一个好的产品，这真是太棒了！

5. We're a high-volume, discount mail-order house.

我们是大批量折扣邮购公司。

实用句型
Practical Sentence Patterns

1 I'd like to ask you some questions. 我想问您一些问题。

2 What benefits can I expect if I exhibit at trade shows? 如果我参加贸易展，能获得什么好处呢？

3 You can use trade shows to promote your products or services. 您可以利用贸易展来推广产品或服务。

4 Can you be more specific? 您能更具体些吗？

5 Trade shows offer you an opportunity to present your products or services to customers face-to-face. 贸易展提供给您一个面对面地向客户展示产品或服务的机会。

6 For an exhibitor, choosing an appropriate trade show is essential. 对于一个参展商，选择一个适当的贸易展是至关重要的。

7 When you attend a trade show, you should make sure what you want to achieve. 当您参加一个贸易展时，您应该明确您想实现什么目标。

8 You should make specific and measurable goals. 您应该制订具体和可衡量的目标。

9 As you know, the Canton Fair is the No. 1 fair in China. 如您所知，广交会是中国第一展。

10 Here is the layout of the exhibition hall and the catalogue. 这是展厅的布局和目录。

11 If you need any other help, please tell us. 如果您需要其他帮助，请告诉我们。

12 After registration, you can begin your visit. 注册后，您就可以开始参观了。

13 Are there any other things you are interested in? 您还有其他感兴趣的事情吗？

14 I am sure you will be able to find some interesting items. 我确信您能发现一些有趣的东西。

15 Thank you for your patience. 谢谢您的耐心。

16 I'm glad to have been of some help to you. 我很高兴对您有所帮助。

实践实训项目
Practical Training Project

I. Building Up Your Vocabulary

1. Match the words on the left with the best translations on the right.

(1) exhibit a. 展览

(2) participate   b. 零件

(3) goal   c. 折扣

(4) benefit   d. 供应

(5) opportunity   e. 具体的

(6) specific   f. 机会

(7) supply   g. 好处

(8) discount   h. 目标

(9) component   i. 参加

(10) measurable   j. 可测量的

2. Complete the following dialogue with proper words or expressions.

A: Good morning. Welcome to _____(上海国际汽车展).

B: Good morning. I have registered as a trade visitor. This is my visitor's card. Where is the _____(接待处), please?

A: This way, please. After registration, you can_____(开始参观).

 (After a few minutes.)

A: OK. Here is_____(参观指南).

B: Very good. Can you give me a _____(简要介绍) about the Shanghai International Auto Show?

A: Well. The Shanghai International Auto Show is actually described as a significant annual automotive event that is well recognized both nationally and internationally. It is _____(很受欢迎) with the media as well as the public.

B: In what way is the show significant for the manufacturers?

A: _____(问得好)! The Auto show is a major marketing event used extensively by the automotive manufacturers to promote their newest cars and trucks and introduce _____(概念车) to the media and the public. You know, some of the vehicles will make their debut on _____(国际市场) at this show.

B: How many halls are there?

A: _____(总共有9个展厅). Which would you like to visit first?

B: I am curious about _____(奥迪和奔驰).

A: _____(请这边走).

B: Thank you.

A: This is_____(奥迪车展位). You see, this is the Audi A8 L6.0 Quattro. It is a high-performance sedan which is equipped with a 6.0-liter W12 engine. With an all-aluminum Space Frame, Audi A8 L6.0 Quattro weighs 300 to 500 pounds less than comparable_____ (豪华轿车).

B: _____(真是太奇妙了)! Audi always emphasizes the design, quality, and comfort issues of the car.

A: Oh, that's Audi TT Clubsport Quattro concept car.

B: Yes. _____(真是难以置信啊)! Let's go and have a look.

II. Substitution Drills

Replace the underlined words with the words in the following boxes.

1. Have you been feeling the itch to send your small business <u>abroad</u>?

> global   worldwide   overseas

2. Many are in your shoes — seeing the <u>benefits</u> of business expansion but also fearing the risk of taking products abroad.

> welfare   returns   gains

3. To begin the international business process, look at <u>potential</u> foreign markets for your business.

> possible   expected   likely

4. The U.S. Department of Commerce website can <u>aid</u> your investigation by giving information about foreign commerce.

> assist   help   lend a hand

5. Also, think of the amount of <u>merchandise</u> you plan on sending to the overseas market.

> goods   items   articles

6. If you find your product is received well, start looking for ways to sell that product <u>permanently</u> in the overseas market.

> timelessly   everlastingly   once and for all

7. China is experiencing a <u>booming</u> economy and has become one of the top picks for exportation.

> prosperous   thriving   flourishing

8. The first is to find a <u>vendor</u> in that country who would be interested in selling your product.

> seller   marketer   trader

9. You can create a partnership with this vendor, giving them a percentage of the <u>profits</u>.

> interests   gains   returns

10. Doing business internationally in this <u>manner</u> is helpful because foreign vendors know how to market to the target culture.

> way   matter   aspect

III. Listening Comprehension

Listen to the dialogue and fill in the blanks according to what you hear. Then practice the dialogue with your partner.

Talking About the Canton Fair

A: Good morning, sir. Welcome to the 119th_____.

B: Good morning, Miss. Wow, what a large crowd! Can you give me a_____ about the Canton Fair?

A: Yes. The Canton Fair is held biannually in_____ every spring and autumn, with a history of 59 years since 1957. The Fair is a_____one with the longest history, the highest level,_____, the most complete exhibit variety, the broadest distribution of overseas buyers, and the greatest business turnover in China.

The Canton Fair _____ more than 24,000 of China's best foreign trade companies with good credibility and sound financial capabilities, and 500 _____companies to participate in the Fair.

Canton Fair is a_____ for import and export mainly, with various and flexible patterns of trade.

Last _____ we had more than 210,000 visitors. This session the number of visitors is expected to increase.

B: You call them visitors, but they are really_____.

A: Yes. As you know, the Canton Fair is the No. 1 fair in China. It has become very important to our_____. There are over 100,000 kinds of famous brand products on display. It features _____ products, specialties, and products adopting advanced technology from various parts of the country.

B: It's great!

A: Yes. You can sit down to have a_____ talk with the sellers in the booth and buy anything you like. Here is the_____of the Exhibition Hall and the catalogue.

B: Thanks a lot.

A: That's all right. If you need any other help, please tell us. We hope you will _____ here.

B: Thank you for your help.

A: My pleasure.

IV. Role Play

Work in pairs or more. Try to act out the following situations.

1. Suppose you are a receptionist at the Canton Fair. Mr. Brown is a first-time visitor and he wants to know more about the Canton Fair.

2. Suppose you are a receptionist at the Canton Fair. John is a VIP. He is going to attend the seminar of the Canton Fair, but he doesn't have any information about the seminar.

Topic: The Feasibility of Establishing a Free Trade Area Between China and South Korea.

Place: Main Hall Meeting Room Pazhou Complex

Time: 9: 00 a.m. to 11: 30 a.m. Today

V. Writing and Speaking

Write one sentence on your own for each of the following words or expressions and speak them out to your partner. Then your partner interprets them into Chinese.

1. promote products

2. offer opportunities

3. present products

4. face-to-face

5. Canton Fair

6. interesting items

会展之窗
The Window of the Convention & Exhibition

10 Tips for Attending a Trade Show

Whether you're seeking to exhibit your products, find vendors, or meet potential customers, a trade show is an excellent place to start. Here are 10 tips for making the most of your next trade show.

Clarify your goals. Before choosing a trade show, decide what you want to achieve — whether it's learning more about your industry, meeting prospects, or buying

inventory. Set measurable goals, such as "Sell X number of products" or "Get 25 qualified leads".

Select the right show. Visit TSNN.com (www.tsnn.com) and *Tradeshow Week* (www.tradeshowweek.com) to search trade shows by industry, date, or location. You can start with your industry's trade show, or ask your colleagues what shows they recommend.

Be prepared. Get as much information as you can in advance. Find out what companies will be exhibiting or attending. Check the show's website for a directory, map, and contact information for exhibitors. Grab a printed directory when you arrive at the show and plan out what you want to see.

Know the rules. If you're exhibiting, ask about details including set-up and breakdown times, size restrictions for your booth and display, wiring and electrical outlets, location and signage, etc. Make a list of what you need to bring — you don't want to find out at the last minute that you're missing one crucial extension cord.

Staff adequately. You need at least two people to man your booth at all times — that way one person can take a quick break. Make sure any employees in your booth are well trained in how to greet attendees and gather information.

Get in shape. Whichever side of the exhibit booth you're on, trade shows are physically demanding. Wear comfortable shoes (you'll be standing or walking all day). Have a quick energy source like nuts or granola bars on hand, and take short breaks when you can.

Meet and greet. Whether you're exhibiting or attending, a friendly attitude is key. Bring more business cards than you think you'll need, and exchange them with everyone you talk to.

Attend events. Trade shows aren't just about exhibits. Be sure to take advantage of the many learning opportunities at the show, such as panel discussions, workshops, or networking sessions.

Stay up late. Don't head to your hotel the minute the show floor closes. Much trade-show business takes place in the evening. Join your new contacts for dinner, attend mixers or hospitality suites, and get to know the people you met during the day.

Follow up. Contact everyone you met at the show within two weeks. You can send information about your business, ask to connect with them on a social networking site, or suggest meeting for coffee or lunch. The goal is to move your relationship forward while the trade show is still fresh in their minds.

Unit Eleven
展会策划
Exhibition Planning

Teaching Targets 教学目标

- To get a general understanding of exhibition planning
- To conduct exhibition planning independently
- To master some useful words, technical terms, phrases, and key sentence patterns
- To hold conversations concerning this topic

背景知识
Background Knowledge

展会策划需要至少提前6个月或更长时间来准备。一份完整的展会策划方案应该包括参展目的、时间流程、预算、空间要求、展台设计和平面设计参数、交流的主要信息、产品和服务展示、所需的现场服务和期限、交通和物流、展台员工的筛选和培训、展前、展中和展后促销活动、展台数据捕捉、评估标准以及后续跟进工作等内容。

热身活动
Warming Up

Listen to the recording carefully and answer the following questions.

1. Why is strategic trade show planning so important?

2. What is the first step in the planning process?

3. How to start the research process?

4. What should you take into consideration when planning a trade show?

示范对话
Model Dialogues

Dialogue 1

(Mr. Li, the general manager of an international exhibition & convention center, is asking Mr. Wang, an exhibition expert, for assistance to prepare for a trade show next year.)

L=Mr. Li; W=Mr. Wang

L: Mr. Wang, a fashion show will be held in June next year. This is the first time for us to organize this type of show. Could you please give me some suggestions?

W: Yes. I think the first and most important step in trade show planning is assembling a team of people with necessary skills and experience. It is greatly important that these people should be great team players and can work responsibly and also think independently.

L: You mean to set up a planning team first?

W: Yes, you might call it a team. The size of your planning team is determined by the size of your show.

L: Then, the next step is?

W: The next step is to appoint a trade show coordinator who will control most of the responsibilities. Since most of the executive decisions will come down to the coordinator's discretion.

L: And, I think the show coordinator should also be a good communicator of ideas with good organizational skills.

W: That's right. The next step is that a budget should be prepared through a thoughtful process.

L: And the coordinator should be in full control of the budget, right?

W: Yes. If payments are approved by someone other than the coordinator, it will be difficult to hold him/her accountable for the expenditures.

L: What's more, choosing a suitable venue is also important in planning a fashion show, right?

W: Yes. This should be arranged as early in the planning process as possible in order to avoid any last minute troubles.

L: What about setting a theme for the show?

W: Setting an appropriate theme for the show is very important, as it will eventually determine the image the public will have of the show. And next is finding exhibitors to take part in the show.

L: You mean to have a promotion?

W: Yes. Sending out personal invitations is probably the most effective way to generate interest. You can also advertise your intention to hold a fashion show in the early months of planning, by using the social or industry groups that are relevant to the type of the show.

L: Thanks for your professional explanation.

W: You are welcome.

Word bank

expert ['ekspɜ:t] *n.* 专家；行家；能手

convention [kən'vɛnʃən] *n.* 大会；协定

assemble [ə'sɛmbl] *v.* 集合，聚集；装配

relevant ['rɛləvənt] *adj.* 相关的；切题的；中肯的

appoint [ə'pɔɪnt] *v.* 任命；指定；约定

coordinator [kəʊ'ɔːdɪneɪtə] *n.* 协调者

budget ['bʌdʒɪt] *n.* 预算；预算费

Notes

1. I think the first and most important step in trade show planning is assembling a team of people with necessary skills and experience.

我认为在展会策划中，第一步，也是最重要的一步，是组建一支拥有必要技能和经验的团队。

2. The size of your planning team is determined by the size of your show.

策划团队的大小是由展会的规模决定的。

3. The next step is that a budget should be prepared through a thoughtful process.

下一步应该深思熟虑地准备预算。

4. Setting an appropriate theme for the show is very important, as it will eventually determine the image the public will have of the show.

必须为展会确立一个合适的主题，因为它将最终决定展会在公众心中的形象。

5. Sending out personal invitations is probably the most effective way to generate interest.

发出私人邀请可能是引起兴趣的最有效的方式。

Dialogue 2

A: Good morning. May I help you?

B: Good morning. I'd like to know something more about your convention and exhibition center. I am looking for a venue to hold an international fashion show.

A: With pleasure. You can ask me any questions about the center.

B: That's very kind of you. Well, I wonder if you've had experience of holding large-scale international fashion shows.

A: Yes. We hold large-scale international fashion shows every year here. This is the largest exhibition and convention center in this province. Please take a look at these photos of the successful events held at our center.

B: Yes, thank you. How far is the center from the international airport?

A: It's just a 15-minute taxi drive and the railway station is about a 10-minute taxi drive.

B: That's great! What about the facilities? And how many exhibition halls are there in the center?

A: We have 25 exhibition halls of different sizes and styles, and all are equipped with modern and functional facilities.

B: Sounds great. What about the services here?

A: We provide our clients with a whole package of services. The staff here are very professional and experienced. They will work with you from the planning of the show to its close, ensuring complete satisfaction.

B: It seems like an ideal venue for our show. Do you have a disk and a brochure that will show me the exhibition spaces?

A: Yes, I can provide you with both, but may I also show you around now?

B: That would be great, thank you.

A: You are welcome.

Word bank

fashion ['fæʃ(ə)n] *n.* 时尚；时装

large-scale ['lɑ: dʒskeɪl] *adj.* 大规模的；大范围的；大比例尺的

facility [fə'sɪləti] *n.* 设施；设备；容易；灵巧

equip [ɪ'kwɪp] *v.* 装备；配备

province ['prɒvɪns] *n.* 省；领域；职权

ensure [ɪn'ʃʊə] *v.* 保证，确保；使安全

professional [prə'feʃənl] *adj.* 专业的；职业的 *n.* 专业人员

ideal [aɪ'dɪəl] *adj.* 理想的；完美的 *n.* 理想；典范

brochure ['brəʊʃə; brɒ'ʃʊə] *n.* 手册，小册子

Notes

1. I am looking for a venue to hold an international fashion show.
   我正在寻找一个场馆来举办国际时装展。

2. I wonder if you've had experience of holding large-scale international fashion shows.
   我想知道您们是否有举办大型国际时装展的经验。

3. We have 25 exhibition halls of different sizes and styles, and all are equipped with modern and functional facilities.

我们有25个不同大小和风格的展厅，所有展厅都配有现代化功能性设施。

4. We provide our clients with a whole package of services.

我们为客户提供一揽子服务。

5. Do you have a disk and a brochure that will show me the exhibition spaces?

您有展示场馆空间的光盘和小册子吗？

实用句型
Practical Sentence Patterns

1 You're going out of your way for us, I believe. 我相信这是对我们的特殊照顾了。

2 It's just the matter of the schedule, that is, if it is convenient for you right now. 如果您们感到方便的话，我想现在讨论一下日程安排的问题。

3 I think we can draw up a tentative plan now. 我认为现在可以先草拟一个临时方案。

4 If you want to make any changes, minor alternations can be made then. 如果您有什么修改意见的话，我们还可以对计划稍加改动。

5 We'll leave some evenings free, that is, if it is all right with you. 如果您们愿意的话，我们想留几个晚上供您们自由支配。

6 I want to know some detailed information about the show. 我想了解一下展会的详细情况。

7 When can we come to decorate our booth? 我们什么时候可以来布置展位？

8 Please reserve a booth for us. We will contact you as soon as we can. 请给我们预留一个展位，我们会尽快联系您们。

9 We would like to register for the show. 我们想报名参加这个展会。

10 This is a great opportunity for us to make our first exhibition. 这是我们第一次参展的好机会。

11 What would be a nice location for our show? 我们的展会在哪里选址比较好呢？

12 Are there any stands available? 还有空余的展位吗？

13 What are the best booths you have? 哪些是您们最好的展位？

14 We provide our clients with the most thoughtful services. 我们为客户提供最周到的服务。

15 It seems like an appropriate venue for our show. 这看起来是一个合适的展会地点。

16 How far is the center from the international airport? 会展中心离国际机场有多远？

实践实训项目
Practical Training Project

I. Building Up Your Vocabulary

1. Match the words on the left with the best translations on the right.

(1) process		a. 展览
(2) convention		b. 小册子
(3) schedule		c. 过程
(4) budget		d. 更改
(5) alternation		e. 会议
(6) expenditure		f. 时间表
(7) facility		g. 预算
(8) brochure		h. 战略的
(9) display		i. 花费
(10) strategic		j. 设施

2. Complete the following sentences with proper words or expressions.

(1) Establish your company's _____(全部的) exhibition strategies.

(2) Research to identify which exhibitions meet your stated_____(目标).

(3) Consider the number and _____(位置) of shows you will attend during the year.

(4) Request information from the sponsors of the shows you are considering. Create a projected annual _____(参展费用).

(5) Determine _____(展览空间) requirements. Book space with the show sponsors.

(6) Rough out an _____(展览计划) with promotional, graphic, and staffing needs.

(7) Set_____ (工作进度表) and completion dates for all show activities.

(8) Confirm progress and _____(交割日) with any outside vendors.

(9) Finalize all_____(旅行安排).

(10) Check that all_____ (展览用品) and materials have been packed or shipped.

(11) Get feedback from the clients about the proposal and confirm the final _____(展览安排).

(12) Present the involved material list and_____ (报价单) of the exhibition.

(13) Confirm the materials and final price. Sign the exhibition cooperation contract, and

prepay the _____(订金).

(14) Prepare all the materials; help the clients _____(处理) the entering documents.

(15) Collect_____ (客户信息), communicate with the clients, and get the exhibition plan.

(16) Make a survey of the _____(展览地点), settle the exhibition agenda, make an exhibition schedule, and present it to the clients for confirmation.

II. Substitution Drills

Replace the underlined words with the words in the following boxes.

1. Participating in trade shows gives you a way to let prospective <u>customers</u> know about your products or services.

| clients | buyers | consumers |

2. Ideally, you will start planning for a <u>trade show</u> at least several months before it begins.

| exhibition | fair | display |

3. This gives you enough time to carefully think about the key messages you want to share with the attendees, create your exhibits, and invite the customers and prospects to visit your <u>booth</u>.

| stand | table | stall |

4. Once you attend your first trade show, <u>evaluate</u> what you'd like to change, and get ready to build upon what you created for the initial show.

| measure | judge | assess |

5. Write down realistic <u>goals</u> for the trade show in which you want to participate, as this will help you figure out what exhibits and staff you need.

| aims | targets | objectives |

6. <u>For instance</u>, you may want to make contact with 150 prospects, or sell $25,000 worth of products, requiring two sales staff on hand at all times.

| for example | as an example |

7. Some companies use trade shows to <u>introduce</u> new products or to help build brand recognition.

| recommend | present | bring out |

8. Most trade shows sell booth space at different prices, <u>depending on</u> where the booth is located and the size.

| based on | according to | in accordance with |

9. If you want to introduce a new product or service, you need the most trafficked spot

you can afford, such as on the <u>main</u> aisle.

| major   chief   central |

10. If you need to <u>convince</u> people to buy by having your sales staff talk to each attendee, choose a quieter space with plenty of room for several sales people to hold conversations with the prospects.

| enable   make   persuade   convict |

III. Listening Comprehension

Listen to the dialogue and fill in the blanks according to what you hear. Then practice the dialogue with your partner.

A: Good morning, Lucy! I'd like you to be involved in a new project.

B: Morning, Charles. What's that? I am all ears.

A: Great! We are planning a new trade show next year, and I want you to work out a project prospectus so as to get the ball rolling (1)_____.

B: I'm only too happy to do it! But you know, Charles, I'm green and (2)_____.

A: No problem, only if you are ready to take the challenge.

B: But how can I start with it?

A: Here are some of the (3)_____ and data for your reference. First of all, set up a main structure of the report, such as the macro political and economic situation, some industrial analysis with key statistics.

B: I see. These are the (4)_____ for the show.

A: Yes. And based on that, you have to find out a number of advantages the show holds. Moreover, I think the show should be positioned as a (5)_____, but with involvement of the general public.

B: This means it opens not only to relevant industrial sectors, but to (6)_____ as well.

A: You are right. In this case, the marketing plan part has to include mass media, some (7)_____ for the society besides professional journals, magazines, and websites.

B: Got it! What about the show (8) _____? Do we have to find some professional associations to be our partners?

A: Of course. You may list several (9)_____ as preliminary organizers, co-organizers, supporters, agents, and something like that.

B: I see. One question, as we don't have any idea about (10)_____, how can I decide

the venue for it?

A: You can list some possible (11)_____as options. We still have to look over available time slots they can offer.

B: How about the (12) _____?

A: You can refer to our previous show for a reference. A final decision will come out after a (13) _____.

B: I understand. When do you need the prospectus?

A: You'd give me the (14)_____ next Friday.

B: I will (15) _____ to get it done then.

IV. Role Play

Work in pairs or more. Try to act out the following situations.

1. Suppose you plan to hold a trade fair. Try to discuss and prepare a timeline for the trade fair.

2. Suppose you are Mr. Brown who is from an international high-tech company and you need to search for a venue to hold a trade fair. You are talking with Miss Li, who is from an exhibition center, to get more detailed information about the center.

V. Writing and Speaking

Write one sentence on your own for each of the following words or expressions and speak them out to your partner. Then your partner interprets them into Chinese.

1. assemble a team

2. set a theme

3. draw up a plan

4. budget

5. a whole package of services

会展之窗
The Window of the Convention & Exhibition

Planning a Trade Show: Strategies for Making a Great Impression

Planning for a trade show is essential to your businesses' success at the event. Any major trade show requires considerable preparation at least a few months in advance, and if you aren't ready, it is certain to present a logistical nightmare. It is very important to develop a solid plan, partner with the right resources, and monitor the process vigilantly.

Participating in a trade show can require a major investment of time, money, and resources. Therefore, you should be critical in your evaluation of which shows are going to benefit your business the most. Consider whether or not the attendees are in your target market or are even likely to be your future customers or clients. Exposure to a couple hundred qualified targets is a far better investment than exposure to thousands of generalized visitors who may not be interested in what you have to offer — unless that is your goal in the first place. You should also specify the things you want to accomplish as a result of your participation in each particular trade show you are evaluating. Do you want to gain exposure to the potential customers, increase your visibility in the community, or check out the competition?

If you want to have a significant presence at a strategic or influential show, you should plan to set up a booth — on your own or with a key partner who will complement your efforts and message. Booth space is usually limited and must be reserved in advance. There is most likely a fee for the space, and can include the square footage, location on the exhibition floor, but may or may not include additional materials such as tables, chairs, or dividers. Developing a good design and clear message for your booth is key to the success of your presence at a trade show. Your area should be inviting, easy to access, and attracting positive attention, and your logo should be big enough to be visible from a distance. You should also employ a dress code for your staff at the show so they will be easily identifiable. This can be a full uniform, or even something as simple as a shirt or hat of the same color. Your staff should also know what is expected of them, and you should brief them on what message you are trying to convey and what aspects should be emphasized, as well as provide the knowledge of how to run any demos or presentations. Nothing looks more unprofessional than demos that don't work, or an uncoordinated work team.

Article Source:

http://strictlybusinessomaha.com/features/planning-a-tradeshow-strategies-for-making-a-great-impression/

Unit Twelve

展会营销与推广
Exhibition Marketing & Promotion

 Teaching Targets 教学目标

- To know the importance of exhibition marketing and promotion
- To improve the listening and speaking skills for exhibition marketing and promotion
- To master some useful words, technical terms, phrases, and key sentence patterns
- To hold conversations concerning this topic

背景知识
Background Knowledge

　　展会营销与推广是指企业通过参加展会活动，利用展会平台展示产品、推广品牌、拓展市场，从而达到营销与推广目标的过程。此过程以展会为载体，以有效的营销、推广手段为支撑，实现企业与参展商、观众等利益相关者的互动，从而推广产品，提升品牌形象，实现商业目标。

　　展会营销与推广具有展示性、互动性、综合性等特点，不仅涉及产品展示、宣传推广等环节，还需要考虑展会的策划、组织、实施、服务等各个环节。

热身活动
Warming Up

Listen to the recording carefully and answer the following questions.

1. What are the two categories of the best tips for trade show giveaways?
2. What kind of promotional items should be chosen?
3. What are the ways to increase foot traffic?
4. Can special events be held at the booth during the trade show?
5. Do trade show giveaways also help promote brand awareness?

示范对话
Model Dialogues

Dialogue 1

A: Good morning. Can I speak to Miss Liu, the marketing manager of Daqi, please?

B: Speaking, please. Who's that?

A: This is James Thompson, the sales manager of Weifeng Group, an international convention and exhibition company. I am calling to see if you are interested in attending the 16th Asia Pet Expo.

B: We'd love to. But we have never done any business through attending any exhibitions before.

A: You will not regret attending the exhibitions. If you want to maximize the investment and make the most of the prospective business, an exhibition provides a unique opportunity to gain exposure to a great many of the potential clients.

B: Yes, I agree.

A: Besides, in the exhibitions, you can enhance brand awareness, build strategic relationships, and obtain or grow your market share with new prospects.

B: I see. Attending exhibitions is a good way to do advertisement. But how do I reach my trade show objectives?

A: Crafting solid messages is an integral part of reaching trade show objectives. Besides, you can connect with your target audience to communicate clearly the distinctive value your company brings.

B: Thank you very much. I want to confirm some details. The exhibition dates are from May 15th to 18th, and the venue is Shanghai International Exhibition Center, right?

A: Yes, you are right. Would you please tell me your email address? I can send you the exhibition prospectus and other materials if you need.

B: OK. My email address is 748736891@qq.com.

A: OK. I have got it. And please understand that the deadline for registration is the end of next month.

B: Thanks. I will visit your website and register as soon as possible.

A: You're welcome. Goodbye.

Word bank

maximize ['mæksɪmaɪz] *v.* 最大化；达到最大值

investment [ɪn'ves(t)m(ə)nt] *n.* 投资；投入

prospective [prə'spektɪv] *adj.* 预期的；未来的

unique [juː'niːk] *adj.* 独特的，独一无二的

exposure [ɪk'spəʊʒə; ek-] *n.* 暴露；曝光；揭露

enhance [ɪn'hɑːns; -hæns; en-] *v.* 提高；加强；增加

brand [brænd] *n.* 商标，牌子

awareness [ə'weənəs] *n.* 意识，认识

confirm [kən'fɜːm] *v.* 确认；确定

prospectus [prə'spektəs] *n.* 内容说明书

registration [redʒɪ'streɪʃ(ə)n] *n.* 登记；注册

Notes

1. If you want to maximize investment and make the most of prospective business, an exhibition provides a unique opportunity to gain exposure to a high volume of potential clients.

如果您想要使投资和预期业务达到最大化收益，展会提供了一个将公司曝光给大量潜在客户的独特的机会。

2. Besides, in the exhibitions, you can enhance brand awareness, build strategic relationships, and obtain or grow your market share with new prospects.

此外，在展会中，您能够提升品牌知名度，建立战略关系，以新的机会获得或增加市场份额。

3. Besides, you can connect with your target audience to communicate clearly the distinctive value your company brings.

此外，您可以与目标客户建立联系以清楚地传递贵公司的独特价值。

4. I can send you the exhibition prospectus and other materials if you need.

如果您需要，我可以把展会说明和其他资料发给您。

5. I will visit your website and register as soon as possible.

我会访问您的网站并尽快注册。

Dialogue 2

Z: Nowadays everything is changing, so is marketing.

X: Yes. Traditional marketing is changing: the customers are getting more and more experienced. Furthermore, they tend to be more price sensitive and may provide word-of-mouth advertising. At the same time, traditional marketing tools are less effective than in the past.

Z: You said it. Advertising is expensive and less effective and the cost of sales personnel is rising. How can we create, win, and dominate markets today? Could you please give us some advice?

X: Yes. I'd be glad to. I suggest that you focus on the services both the exhibitors and attendees perceive as valuable.

Z: What does that mean?

X: That means you need to live and breathe for your customers. It's the first step to make your marketing job possible.

Z: It is very important to make our marketing mode different from others, right?

X: Right. If you always follow others, you'll become stale, and will never win against your competitors. Since the attendees expect to see and experience something new and exciting from visiting the exhibitors' booths, the changes have to be in line with the essence of your show.

Z: How can we effectively touch the exhibitors' hearts with our show promotion?

X: There are some ways.

Z: Could you give me an example in detail?

X: You may use information technology, brands, and integrated communications and entertainment. Have you heard of "experiential marketing"?

Z: No. What is it?

X: It is the latest trend in marketing that focuses on the experiences of the customers. It can help to stimulate excitement among your exhibitors and attendees that your show is an experience not to be missed.

Z: It is really a good idea. I'd better tell my team about it. Thank you so much for your advice.

X: You are welcome.

Word bank

sensitive ['sensɪtɪv] *adj.* 敏感的；灵敏的；易受影响的

word-of-mouth ['wə: dəv'mauθ] *adj.* 口头的，口述的

dominate ['dɒmɪneɪt] *v.* 控制；支配；占优势

stale [steɪl] *adj.* 陈腐的；没有新意的

competitor [kəm'petɪtə] *n.* 竞争者，对手

essence ['es(ə)ns] *n.* 本质，实质；精华

integrate ['ɪntɪgreɪt] *v.* 使……完整；使……成为整体

entertainment [entə'teɪnm(ə)nt] *n.* 娱乐；消遣；款待

stimulate ['stɪmjʊleɪt] *v.* 刺激；鼓舞，激励

Notes

1. Furthermore, they tend to be more price sensitive and may provide word-of-mouth advertising.

而且，他们往往对价格更敏感，并且可能提供口碑宣传。

2. Advertising is expensive and less effective and the cost of sales personnel is rising.

广告很贵，效果不好并且销售人员的成本在增加。

3. How can we create, win, and dominate markets today?

如今，我们如何能够创造、赢得和占有市场呢？

4. I suggest that you focus on the services both the exhibitors and attendees perceive as valuable.

我建议您专注于参展商和观众都认为有价值的服务。

5. If you always follow others, you'll become stale, and will never win against your competitors.

如果您总是步人后尘，您就会变得没有新意，就永远不会战胜您的竞争对手。

实用句型
Practical Sentence Patterns

1 I am calling to see if you are interested in attending the 16th Asia Pet Expo. 我打电话是想看看您是否有兴趣参加第16届亚洲宠物展览会。

2 Attending exhibitions is a good way to do advertisement. 参加展览是一种很好的宣传方式。

3 Good quality and low price will help push the sales of our products. 良好的质量和低廉的价格将有助于我们产品的销售。

4 Let me show you some of the great features of our newest products. 让我向您展示我们最新产品的一些优越特性。

5 This price is not our regular price. It is a special promotion. 这个价格不是我们的正常价格，是特别促销价。

6 We have a lot of products for your choice. 我们有很多产品供您选择。

7 This type of machine is top of the line. 这款机器是同类产品中最好的。

8 If you have any questions, we can provide technical support to you. 如果您有什么问题，我们可以提供技术上的支持。

9 We will provide free samples to our potential customers. 我们会给潜在客户免费提供样品。

10 If you are not satisfied with our products, you can get a full refund. 如果您对我们的产品不满意，可以获得全额退款。

11 In recent times, everything is changing, and so is marketing. 在当今时代，一切都在

变化，市场营销也是如此。

⓬ At the same time, traditional or old-style marketing tools are less effective than in the past. 与此同时，传统或老式的营销手段已经渐渐失去效果了。

实践实训项目
Practical Training Project

I. Building Up Your Vocabulary

1. Match the words on the left with the best translations on the right.

(1) exposure	a. 娱乐
(2) marketing	b. 赠品
(3) competitor	c. 商标
(4) dominate	d. 促销
(5) word-of-mouth	e. 曝光
(6) giveaway	f. 控制
(7) brand	g. 登记
(8) entertainment	h. 口碑
(9) registration	i. 竞争者
(10) promotion	j. 营销

2. Complete the following sentences with proper words or expressions.

(1) Business-to-business marketers actually invest more money on trade shows than any other _____ (营销手段).

(2) The first step in planning your trade show successfully is to set _____ (有效的和现实的) trade show objectives and measurements for them.

(3) Effectively planning your show's _____ (目标) allows the rest of your show to fall into place.

(4) Choosing the right measurement tools enables you to _____ (得出正确的结论) following your trade show performance.

(5) Once you know the reason you are exhibiting, set objectives based on them that you can measure — and then _____ (评估) and report them.

(6) Exhibiting can be complex. A large part of that challenge is to identify how much to budget for _____ (相关服务).

(7) To start_____(选择) the shows you want to exhibit at only after you have set your trade show objectives.

(8) Trade show _____(促销) are the secret weapon of the veteran trade show manager. That's because, when done right, trade show promotions work so well.

(9) _____(展会员工) is uncomfortable for almost everyone at first.

(10) By tracking your results from show to show, you can make_____(精明的决策) about which shows to continue, expand, contract, or cut.

II. Substitution Drills

Replace the underlined words with the words in the following boxes.

1. Trade show promotions drive more traffic to your booth.

| advertising | marketing | publicizing | propaganda |

2. Giveaways are worthwhile because they get more people to enter your trade show exhibit and help you be remembered after the show.

| freebies | small gifts | samples |

3. Promotions are great conversation starters — but your booth staff have to keep the conversation going, rather than let the prospect walk off.

| talk | communication | dialogue |

4. Discounts and show specials help you close the deal when you get rare face-to-face time with hard-to-reach prospects.

| price reductions | deductions | rebates |

5. Before the show, reach out to the attendees at minimum with email that offers something of value, potentially with direct mail, and for top prospects, by personal telephone calls.

| provides | gives | supplies | shows |

6. Put more effort into social media for trade show promotions — but only when you are already maximizing traditional pre-show and at-show promotions.

| old | conventional | previous | former |

7. Your social media efforts should be proportionate to the social-media adaption rate of your target audience.

| aim | objective | specific |

8. Giveaways that tie into your marketing message are much more memorable after the show.

| unforgettable | impressive | durable |

9. Success at a trade show requires finding a way to capture the attention of the largest

number of attendees.

| catch   obtain   gain   attract |

10. Nothing can catch the eye like light, sound, and motion. If you want to make the most of your trade show opportunity, you need to tap into the technology <u>available</u>.

| obtainable   valid   effective   easy to get |

III. Listening Comprehension

Listen to the dialogue and fill in the blanks according to what you hear. Then practice the dialogue with your partner.

A: Good morning. What can I do for you?

B: Yes. My name is Josh Smith. I'm from an international high-tech company in Shanghai. I would like to know something about_____in your center.

A: I'm glad to be _____. What would you like to know?

B: Could you give a _____ about what type of advertising you are offering?

A: Sure. We offer exhibitors an opportunity to advertise their products and gain exposure to the attendees by placing a poster banner at the _____ to the show.

B: Do you offer per show advertising or _____advertising?

A: Both. For per show advertising, locations are available at our _____. You may place your company's name and list your products, along with your booth number, to invite the attendees to visit you inside.

B: What about annual advertising?

A: Your advertising will be placed in a _____ location for one year. During the time, you may change your ad twice in order to introduce your new products.

B: Good. What about advertising through the _____?

A: That's also a good way for your marketing _____.

B: How many _____ do you have on your website each month?

A: 20,000 hits last year each month. But this year it_____ 26,000 hits each month.

B: How can we advertise on your website?

A: You may _____a banner ad or a link to your own website.

B: Very good. Thank you for your introduction. We will come back after I give the information to our _____.

A: You are welcome. We look forward to seeing you again.

IV. Role Play

Work in pairs or more. Try to act out the following situations.

1. Suppose you are a sales executive and you are introducing the tools of marketing before a trade show to the members of the sales department.

2. Suppose you are Mr. Brown who comes from a company that produces beauty products. The company is going to attend a Featured Health & Beauty Trade Show. You are talking with Mr. Zhang, an advertising agent, about how to make advertisements about the products and how to attract more customers.

V. Writing and Speaking

Write one sentence on your own for each of the following words or expressions and speak them out to your partner. Then your partner interprets them into Chinese.

1. business-to-business

2. measurement tools

3. indoor advertising

4. outdoor advertisement

5. Internet advertising

会展之窗
The Window of the Convention & Exhibition

Planning Your Marketing Strategy

Well planned and executed trade show promotions are essential to fully benefit from event participation and achieve your exhibiting goals.

For exhibit marketing to be effective, you must have specific objectives to measure success and have determined the role trade shows will play, as part of your overall sales and marketing plan.

Moreover, finding opportunistic shows that reach your target audience, along with having well-designed, memorable trade show exhibits, messages, and promotional products, is essential to set the stage for successful outcomes.

Effective trade show marketing includes a multi-phased strategy. This approach encompasses a variety of marketing channels to attract visitors to your trade show display — and engage both prospects and customers.

There are three phases of trade show promotion.

Phase 1: Personalized contact prior to the event.

Contact conference registrants in advance through personalized phone calls, written invitations, direct mail initiatives, social media, and/or email communications. You may also want to mail out meaningful giveaways along with a personalized letter to introduce your products, share your booth location, and encourage potential buyers to visit your exhibit.

To complement your efforts, be sure to leverage digital media by placing exhibiting information on your website, as well as utilizing social networks and mobile marketing to get the message out.

Phase 2: Marketing activities during the show.

This includes live entertainment, hands-on activities, audio-visual programs, unique booth attractions, interactive games, trade show giveaways, and food. Using social media posts throughout the show also engages attendees and keeps them apprised of what's happening at your booth. Of course, a well-trained, professional, and welcoming trade show team is paramount to success.

Phase 3: Follow up after the show to convert leads into sales.

Send a personalized handwritten note, along with a customized company information packet or other appropriate material, to booth visitors within a week following the trade show event. For top leads, add a personal phone call to make a lasting impression and reinforce your commitment to service.

In this time of intense texting, email, and messaging through social networking sites, a personal phone call to your valued prospects makes a powerful impact and may help solidify the sale. Warm, personal contact is the consistent thread in every aspect of marketing and trade show promotions.

Strong, thoughtful relationship-building strategies before, during, and after the show can effectively separate you from your competitors — and make the difference between generating a lead and making a sale.

Each contact you make reinforces your company's commitment to quality and customer care, which are essential attributes in the competitive marketplace.

In addition, trade show marketing strategies that focus on relationship management and personalized attention are just as important when you are participating in virtual trade shows as they are for traditional, face-to-face events.

Article Source:

http://www.trade-show-advisor.com/trade-show-promotions.html

Unit Thirteen

展会邀请

Trade Show Invitation

Teaching Targets 教学目标

- To learn how to invite people to the exhibition
- To master some useful expressions and sentences
- To hold conversations concerning this topic

背景知识
Background Knowledge

展会邀请是指展会招商、招展邀请，也就是通过各种方式邀请那些对拟办展览会有需要和感兴趣的参展商、采购商和观众参加展览会。参展商和观众是展会成功举办不可或缺的重要因素，拥有一定数量的优质参展商和观众是一个展会成功的重要标志之一。展会成功的关键在于招展和招商。

热身活动
Warming Up

Listen to the recording carefully and answer the following questions.

1. What is essential for holding an exhibition?

2. What is the best way to invite people?

3. Why is an invitation letter important?

4. What should be provided in an invitation letter?

5. What should you pay attention to when writing the letter?

示范对话
Model Dialogues

Dialogue 1

Wang Hong (i.e. W), an assistant of the trade show, calls a regular client, Mr. Brown (i.e. B) of an American company in China to attend their show.

B: Good morning, this is International Optics Company, Mr. Brown speaking. How may I assist you?

W: Good morning, Mr. Brown. This is Wang Hong from Shanghai Trade Show. I haven't seen you for ages! How has your company been going?

B: Pretty well. We're planning to expand our business.

W: Fine. I'm calling to invite you to attend the China (Shanghai) International Optics Fair on March 11th, 2024.

B: We accept with pleasure. We would like to present our new products there.

W: You are warmly welcome. I'm going to send you the schedule, application form, charges, and details of certain other services provided during the period of the trade show.

B: I appreciate that very much.

W: By the way, I suggest that you provide a brief introduction of your company and the main products, written in Chinese and English to the organizing committee. They will publish a special edition about the exhibitors and their products with the link to the website at the same time.

B: That's OK. We'll contact you as soon as possible.

W: OK. I'll email very soon the information I mentioned.

B: Thank you. See you.

W: My pleasure. See you then.

Word bank

client ['klaɪənt] *n.* 客户；顾客

optics ['ɒptɪks] *n.* [光] 光学

expand [ɪk'spænd] *v.* 扩张，扩大

fair [feə] *n.* 展览会；市集

schedule ['ʃedjuːl; 'sked-] *n.* 时间表；计划表

application [ˌæplɪ'keɪʃ(ə)n] *n.* 申请

appreciate [ə'priːʃɪeɪt] *v.* 欣赏；感激

brief [briːf] *adj.* 简短的，简洁的

committee [kə'mɪtɪ] *n.* 委员会

exhibitor [ɪg'zɪbɪtə] *n.* 参展商

Notes

1. How may I assist you?
   有什么能帮您吗?

2. We're planning to expand our business.
   我们打算拓展业务。

3. I'm calling to invite you to attend the China (Shanghai) International Optics Fair

on March 11th, 2024.

我打电话是想邀请您参加2024年3月11日举行的中国(上海)国际眼镜业展览会。

4. I'm going to send you the schedule, application form, charges, and details of certain other services provided during the period of the trade show.

我会把日程安排、申请表、费用详情以及展会期间提供的其他服务的详细情况寄给您。

5. I'll email very soon the information I mentioned.

我很快会将提到的信息用邮件发给您。

Dialogue 2

A potential exhibitor, Mr. Black (i.e. B), telephones the trade show to ask for information. Ms. Li (i.e. L), an assistant of the show, answers the phone call.

B: Good morning. I'm calling because I saw your ad on the official website this morning about your trade show.

L: Thank you. Let me give you some detailed information about it. The trade fair will be held in Shanghai, China, from February 24th to February 26th, 2024. If you want to attend it, you can download the application form from the Internet.

B: OK. How about the deadline for registration?

L: The day after tomorrow. However, we can make exceptions for overseas companies.

B: Where shall I send the registration form and the fee?

L: To the address written at the bottom of the form. Please send it as soon as possible to reserve a booth.

B: How about the sizes of the booths?

L: There are dozens of sizes. Of course the larger ones cost more.

B: Does the price of the show include meals?

L: Yes. It includes three meals a day.

B: Got it. Thank you.

L: You are welcome.

Word bank

potential [pəˈtenʃl] *adj.* 潜在的；可能的

official [əˈfɪʃ(ə)l] *adj.* 官方的；正式的

download [ˌdaʊnˈləʊd] *v.* 下载

registration [redʒɪˈstreɪʃ(ə)n] *n.* 登记；注册

exception [ɪkˈsepʃ(ə)n; ek-] *n.* 例外

address [əˈdres] *n.* 地址

reserve [rɪˈzɜːv] *v.* 预订；储备；保留

booth [buːð; buːθ] *n.* 展位；货摊

Notes

1. Let me give you some detailed information about it.

   请允许我详细介绍这方面的信息。

2. If you want to attend it, you can download the application form from the Internet.

   如果您想参加，请在网上下载申请表格。

3. How about the deadline for registration?

   登记注册的截止日期是什么时候？

4. However, we can make exceptions for overseas companies.

   然而，我们可以为海外公司破例。

5. Please send it as soon as possible to reserve a booth.

   请尽快寄出(申请表)以预订展位。

实用句型
Practical Sentence Patterns

1 It's very honored to meet you. 很荣幸见到您！

2 We're going to update our business. 我们将进行业务升级。

3 We would like to exhibit our newest products at your trade show. 我们想要在您的展会上展示我们的最新产品。

4 We'll contact you as soon as we can. 我们会尽快与您联系。

5 You'll be given a special offer if you register now. 如果您现在注册，可以享受特别优惠价。

6 Are there any booths still available? 还有空的展位吗？

7 Thank you for your kind invitation. 谢谢您的盛情邀请。

8 I believe that we can cooperate in the future. 我相信我们将来可以合作。

⑨ I'm pleased to invite you to be our trade show visitor. 我很高兴邀请您做我们的展会观众。

⑩ I sincerely hope you can join us for the trade show. 我真诚希望您们能参加这次展会。

⑪ What time would be convenient for you? 您什么时候方便呢?

⑫ We're looking forward to hearing from you. 我们期待您的回复。

⑬ I'd like to know something about your exhibition in detail. 我想详细了解您们的展会。

⑭ How about the price for a booth? 展位的价格怎么样?

⑮ Thank you for remembering me. 谢谢您记得我。

⑯ We are going to prepare a guest card for you. 我们将为您准备一张贵宾卡。

实践实训项目
Practical Training Project

I. Building Up Your Vocabulary

1. Match the words on the left with the best translations on the right.

(1) design	a. 折扣
(2) phase	b. 位置
(3) commodity	c. 平均
(4) registration	d. 可利用的
(5) professional	e. 地区
(6) region	f. 专业的
(7) available	g. 登记
(8) average	h. 商品
(9) location	i. 阶段
(10) discount	j. 设计

2. Complete the following dialogue with proper words or expressions.

A: Good morning, this is Top Fashion Design_____ (有限公司), Mr. Smith speaking. Can I help you?

B: Good morning, Mr. Smith. This is Wang Fang from Beijing Trade Show. _____(好久不见)! How has your company been doing?

A: Pretty good. We're going to _____ (拓展业务).

B: Great, I am very glad to hear this good news from you. I'm calling to invite you to attend the 15th Beijing _____ (国际时装秀) on May 8th, 2024.

A: We can accept your invitation with great pleasure. We would like to _____ (展示我们的新产品) at your show.

B: You are warmly welcome. I'm going to send you the schedule, _____ (申请表), charges, and details of other services provided during the show.

A: Thanks very much.

B: By the way, I suggest that you provide a _____ (简介) of your company including the main products, written in both Chinese and English, and submit it to our Organizing Committee. They will publish a special edition that will detail the exhibitors and their products with the link to the show website.

A: No problem. _____ (我们会尽快联系您).

B: OK. I'll email the information I mentioned ahead to you.

A: Thank you so much for contacting me.

B: My pleasure. See you at the show.

II. Substitution Drills

Replace the underlined words with the words in the following boxes.

1. Planning <u>ahead</u> and pre-show outreach are extremely important.

in advance   previously   beforehand

2. A trade show can be extremely lively, busy, and distracting which means that if you take the time to create a clean and warm <u>environment</u> that you can invite people into it, it is more likely to be well received than if you were yelling at them or shining flashy objects at their faces.

circumstance   surrounding   condition

3. You can also drive traffic to your booth by <u>offering</u> incentives.

affording   giving   providing

4. <u>Launch</u> your new products during the trade shows; if you don't have anything new, make sure you promote some kind of special offer or even a gift just for stopping by.

release   send   bring out

5. The old strategy of drawing names or business cards from a bowl is <u>outdated</u>, and the

best way to generate real leads is to have actual conversations establishing relationships.

old　out-of-date　obsolete

6. You will need to have signs and posters to <u>announce</u> your trade show displays, which means you will need a place to print those things off.

inform　declare　proclaim

7. These skills help them as human beings to better communicate, have less stress, feel more <u>fulfilled</u>, and be safer.

content　satisfactory　completed

8. Interoffice communication is one of the great <u>corporate</u> challenges.

collective　common　universal

9. This letter acts as a personal request to others and is an <u>affectionate</u> way to enhance your contacts and business.

warm　lovesome　heartful　tender

10. These letters should be in a humble tone and should show <u>gratitude</u>.

thanks　appreciation　thankfulness

III. Listening Comprehension

Listen to the dialogue and fill in the blanks according to what you hear. Then practice the dialogue with your partner.

A: Good morning, _____ of Gems & Jewellery Trade Show in China. How can I help you?

B: Good morning, I'm _____ of HD Jewellery Design Co. Ltd. I'd like to know something about your exhibition in May.

A: Well, the exhibition is about to _____ on May 16th. We have two phases for different commodities. The attendance will be the largest ever because we have received _____ for the exhibition from many factories and enterprises and we expect to have about 2000 _____ from 150 countries and regions.

B: Are there any booths still _____?

A: Yes, we still have some _____. I would like to advise you to book very soon before they are all gone.

B: How about the price for a booth?

A: The average price of a _____ is $3,200, but the price varies according to the size and location.

B: Could we have some_____?

A: Of course. We will give you a good discount if you_____now.

B: Thank you. We'll register now. And the deposit will be credited to your account

_____. As for the exact booth, we will_____ to talk it over.

A: OK. I will be sure to _____ some good ones to you.

IV. Role Play

Work in pairs or more. Try to act out the following situation.

Suppose you are an assistant of China (Shanghai) International Fashion Show. You are calling one of your regular clients to invite him to attend your trade show from May 26th to 28th, 2024.

V. Writing and Speaking

Write one sentence on your own for each of the following words or expressions and speak them out to your partner. Then your partner interprets them into Chinese.

1. Organizing Committee

2. professional buying groups

3. vacant booths

4. average price

5. guest card

6. warmly welcome

会展之窗
The Window of the Convention & Exhibition

Extend an Invitation to Attend a Trade Show, Seminar, or Conference

Sample #1

Do you need just a few more job skills to make you more marketable? Attend Doe's Job Skill Seminar and learn several invaluable skills guaranteed to better your present situation or help you find a job. Just a phone call away.

Here are six reasons to sign up today:

*(List six prominent features.)

Nine out of ten of Doe's Job Skill students have advanced to better employment.

Contact me today to enroll in my (date) class. Call 555-5555.

P.S. You can never be too qualified.

Sample #2

Do you have what it takes to become certified in the ski patrol?

Attend my accelerated course, and you'll be wearing the uniform in no time. It's a terrific job for someone who loves skiing. The satisfaction is unsurpassed, and you get to do what you love — ski.

In the course, you'll learn:

*(List some prominent features.)

Don't miss this exciting opportunity to become certified in the ski patrol. Fill out the enclosed reply card to secure your spot in the upcoming session.

Sample #3

Discover how you can make MORE MONEY than you ever dreamed of.

Please accept this invitation to a FREE SEMINAR in (location, date, time).

It will only take 60 minutes, but those minutes will be packed with information on how you can become rich in a very short period of time. We'll teach you how to:

*(List some prominent features of your program.)

How can all this be done? By simply understanding the dynamics of stock trading.

You may say, "But I don't know the first thing about stocks." No problem. This informative seminar teaches you the basics. So pick up the phone right now and phone this number for your reservation: 555-5555.

You won't be sorry, believe me.

P.S. The seminar presenter will be John Doe. The former attendees say that "John Doe is one of the most knowledgeable speakers they've ever heard." Give us a call today.

Sample #4

Your crafts hobby can be a profitable part-time business.

That's right! Many crafts enthusiasts have found that there's no better or more enjoyable way to make money than with their crafts. Imagine earning thousands of dollars doing what you love to do.

Sign up today for our exciting seminar, "Making Your Hobby a Money-maker". We'll show you the five simple steps for turning your hobby into a lucrative part-time business.

You'll learn from the pros such things as:

* (List 5 or more prominent features.)

* And much more!

Call today! Mail the enclosed card and we'll send you informative literature explaining the seminar in detail.

To receive the literature, our seminar registration form, and a FREE listing of craft fairs, mail the card now.

You have no obligation. If you decide not to attend, you may keep the FREE listing of craft fairs as our gift.

Sample #5

One benefit that companies often provide their employees is seminars on life skills. These skills go beyond skills that they must develop for their jobs; these skills help them as human beings to better communicate, have less stress, feel more fulfilled, and be safer.

Doe Living Skills conducts such courses on a variety of subjects. Some include:

*(List several prominent subjects.)

An employee who is happier and progressing personally is one who will do his job better. Our instructor can present these courses at your office or at another location of your choice. And the price is very affordable.

Please read over the enclosed brochure. I'll be happy to contact you next week to answer any questions and perhaps set up an appointment. I hope you will consider making this exceptional opportunity available to your employees!

Sample #6

Have you ever heard, "My boss doesn't make himself clear... I thought he said..."? As the director of human resources for your company, you probably hear things like this daily. Interoffice communication is one of the great corporate challenges. How your employees communicate with co-workers and clients greatly impacts on the success of your business.

Doe Executive Education can help your staff improve their communication skills. We offer a one-day workshop, which, until recently has been available only to mega-corporations. We focus on:

*(List several prominent features of your workshop.)

Enclosed is some explanatory information and a list of our clients. I will call you next week to answer any questions. We look forward to serving you.

Article Source:

http://www.writeexpress.com/invita17.html

Unit Fourteen

展品介绍

Introduction to Exhibits

Teaching Targets 教学目标

- To learn to make an introduction to the exhibits
- To attract customers with an effective product introduction
- To master some useful expressions & sentences
- To hold conversations concerning this topic

背景知识
Background Knowledge

展品介绍是公司客户代表本着销售产品的目的向客户宣讲以展示公司的产品和服务的活动。展品介绍是营销过程中很重要的部分，因为在此环节公司客户代表能够直接在展会上开展营销活动，形成了个性化的销售方式。

热身活动
Warming Up

Listen to the recording carefully and answer the following questions.

1. Why can attracting and retaining customers be simple or difficult?

2. Why does a business have to provide products that will satisfy the customers?

3. What is less known about product selling?

4. What's the key to attracting customers?

示范对话
Model Dialogues

Dialogue 1

Mr. Wu, an assistant of Shanghai Silk Group Co. Ltd., is receiving a foreign business man, Mr. Brown. They are talking about the quality of the products.

W=Wu; B=Mr. Brown

W: Good morning, sir. Welcome to our display. Would you like to have a look at the catalogue and see what products you are interested in?

B: Yes, please. We know that Chinese silk is very popular for its superior quality and competitive price. Could you give me a detailed description of your products?

W: Let me introduce our products to you. We have a variety of Chinese silk articles here. They are divided into different types: silk garments, silk decoration items, and silk fashion accessories including silk pajamas, silk scarves, silk tassels, silk cravats, etc. What about having a look at our samples?

B: I am dazzled by so many types of silk products.

W: Which item do you think might find a ready market in your country?

B: I'm thinking about the pajama series.

W: That is a good idea! They are soft to touch and are 100% pure silk. These products have been sold in a number of areas abroad.

B: Good. The quality and variety of your products are very attractive. How do you ensure quality control?

W: Well, it's done by the quality control department. Final inspection is done by our experts. We guarantee world-standard quality.

B: If your products are of such high quality, then the price must be high.

W: Actually, that's not the case. We are fully aware of the importance of price. In order to keep our prices down, we try to cut our costs wherever possible.

Word bank

superior [su:'pɪərɪə; sju:-] *adj.* 上乘的

competitive [kəm'petɪtɪv] *adj.* 竞争的；有竞争力的

description [dɪ'skrɪpʃ(ə)n] *n.* 描述，描写；类型；说明书

article ['ɑ:tɪk(ə)l] *n.* 货品；物品

decoration [dekə'reɪʃ(ə)n] *n.* 装饰，装潢；装饰品

accessory [ək'ses(ə)rɪ] *n.* 配件；附件

pajama [pə'dʒɑ:mə] *n.* 睡衣

tassel ['tæs(ə)l] *n.* 流苏；缨；穗

cravat [krə'væt] *n.* 领带；领巾，领结

dazzle ['dæz(ə)l] *v.* 使……目眩

standard ['stændəd] *n.* 标准；水准 *adj.* 标准的

Notes

1. Would you like to have a look at the catalogue and see what interests you?

您要不要看一下产品目录，看看您对什么产品感兴趣？

2. We understand that Chinese silk is very popular for its superior quality and competitive price.

我们都知道中国丝绸由于上乘的品质和具有竞争力的价格而很受欢迎。

3. Could you give me a detailed description of your products?

您能够详细地描述一下您的产品吗?

4. I am dazzled by so many types of silk products.

这么多种类的丝织品让我眼花缭乱。

5. Which item do you think might find a ready market in your country?

您认为哪个产品在您们国家会很有销路?

Dialogue 2

A staff member is showing James around the product exhibition room.

S=staff member; J=James

S: Would you like to have a look at our display room?

J: Yes. That would be a good idea.

S: This way, please.

J: Quite a selection!

S: Where shall we start? You may be interested in only some of the items. Let's look at those.

J: Good idea!

S: Have you been in the textile business for a long time?

J: Yes. I've been in textiles for about 40 years. The company has been in business since 1985.

S: No wonder you're so experienced.

J: The textile business has become more difficult since the competition grew.

S: That's true.

J: Do you have a catalog or something that tells me about your company?

S: Yes. I will get you some later.

J: Thanks. When can we discuss some details?

S: Would tomorrow be convenient?

J: Yes. That'll be fine.

Word bank

item ['aɪtəm] *n.* 一件商品(或物品)

textile ['tekstaɪl] *n.* 纺织品，织物 *adj.* 纺织的

competition [kɒmpɪ'tɪʃ(ə)n] *n.* 竞争；比赛，竞赛

catalog ['kætəlɒg] *n.* 目录；产品目录

convenient [kən'viːnɪənt] *adj.* 方便的

Notes

1. Would you like to have a look at our product exhibition room?

   您愿意看看我们的产品展厅吗?

2. Have you been in the textile business a long time?

   您做纺织品生意已经很长时间了吧?

3. I've been in textiles for about 40 years. The company has been in business since 1985.

   我做纺织品这一行已经有40来年了。公司从1985年开始运营。

4. The textile business has become more difficult since the competition grew.

   由于竞争加剧，纺织品生意越来越难做。

5. When can we discuss some details?

   我们什么时候能够讨论一下细节?

实用句型
Practical Sentence Patterns

🔟 Could you give me a detailed description of your products? 您能给我详细地描述您的产品吗?

🔟 Let me introduce our products to you. 让我为您介绍一下我们的产品。

🔟 The quality and variety of your products are very attractive. 您们产品的质量和品种非常有吸引力。

🔟 If your products are of such high quality, then the price must be high. 如果您们的产品质量高，价格也一定高。

🔟 Welcome to our display area. 欢迎来到我们的展区。

6 Because of the high cost of railway transportation, we prefer sea transportation. 因为铁路运输费用高，我们宁愿走海运。

7 I want to take a look at your cutting tools. 我想看看您的切割工具。

8 Let me show you how to operate this. 让我告诉您如何操作。

9 I love Chinese traditional handicrafts and they are very popular in my country. 我爱中国传统手工艺品，它们在我的国家很受欢迎。

10 Our prices vary because the material, design, and craftsmanship are different. 我们的价格有所不同，因为材料、设计和工艺是不同的。

11 Would you please leave your contact number so that we can provide you with the latest information? 请留下您的联系电话，以便我们为您提供最新的信息，好吗？

12 This is my business card with my name and telephone number. 这是我的名片，上面有我的名字和电话号码。

13 Can you give me some suggestions? You are so experienced. 您经验丰富，能给我一些建议吗？

14 Each time when you meet a new client, modify your presentation to satisfy his particular needs. 每当您遇到一个新客户的时候都要修改您的演示，以满足客户的特殊需求。

15 You should always present the key points and the features of the products to the clients at first. 您应该首先向客户介绍产品的关键点和特征。

16 Today's business people are too busy to listen to long-winded introduction. 今天的商业人士都太忙，没有时间听冗长的介绍。

17 We should try to provide convenience for our clients. 我们应该努力为我们的客户提供方便。

18 You can try to vary your voice and tone, and use some relaxing words and gestures. A monotone should be avoided. 您可以试着改变您的声音和音调并使用一些令人放松的语言和手势，以避免单调。

实践实训项目
Practical Training Project

I. Building Up Your Vocabulary

1. Match the words on the left with the best translations on the right.

    (1) retain   a. 保持

(2) ultimately		b. 使目眩
(3) fulfill		c. 最终地
(4) superior		d. 样品
(5) description		e. 高级的
(6) item		f. 实现
(7) competitive		g. 方便的
(8) convenient		h. 描述
(9) dazzle		i. 有竞争力的
(10) sample		j. 商品

2. Complete the following dialogue with proper words or expressions.

A: Good morning, welcome to our booth.

B: Good morning.

A: I'm Andrew Wang from Daxing_____ (传统手工艺品) Company. I'm sure you will be interested in our products.

B: That's right. I love Chinese traditional handicrafts and they are_____ (很受欢迎) in my country.

A: That's great! We have come here to _____ (展示) some of the Chinese traditional handicrafts our company makes. There's a great variety to choose from. You'll surely find_____ (一些有趣的东西). Please come here and I'll show you what we have.

B: Thank you very much. Could you show me _____ (特别的东西)?

A: Certainly. Here is a fine collection of Chinese traditional handicrafts. They are all _____ (手工制造).

B: Really? That's fantastic! How about the prices?

A: Well, our prices vary because the material, design, and _____ (技艺) are different. This is a complete set of our latest _____ (目录) together with a price list for your consideration. Would you please leave your _____ (联系电话) so that we can provide you with the latest information?

B: Sure. This is my_____ (名片) with my name and telephone number.

A: Thank you. This is my card. You can contact us any time.

B: Fine, thank you.

A: You are welcome.

II. Substitution Drills

Replace the underlined words with the words in the following boxes.

1. An effective sales introduction not only educates <u>prospective</u> customers about your products or services, but it also explains how you can meet a customer's specific needs and help him achieve his goals.

| potential   expected   future |

2. Creating a successful sales introduction <u>requires</u> thorough research and careful preparation.

| needs   demands   should have |

3. Time <u>invested</u> in doing your homework will lead to a higher percentage of closed sales.

| used   put   given   devoted |

4. Plan your research process and <u>devise</u> a system for keeping all of your information organized.

| design   come up with   conceive |

5. Keep separate <u>files</u> for product information, company information, and details about your prospective customers.

| papers   documents   materials |

6. Create an organized filing system and naming conventions for your files so you can <u>access</u> them as needed.

| use   make use of   employ |

7. Research the products or services you are selling <u>thoroughly</u>. Learn about the products inside and out, and strive to keep abreast of any new developments.

| completely   entirely   absolutely   totally |

8. <u>Compel</u> your customers to invest in you because of the higher value you offer.

| make   enable   force |

9. Learn the <u>features</u> of your products or services and the potential benefits to your specific customers.

| characteristics   specialities   strengths |

10. Have an <u>exhaustive</u> understanding about how the products are manufactured and packaged.

| detailed   thorough   full |

III. Listening Comprehension

Listen to the dialogue and fill in the blanks according to what you hear. Then practice the dialogue with your partner.

A: Are you interested in our _____? What can I do for you?

B: This is really nice!

A: This is our newly _____ product. Would you like to see it?

B: Yes, please.

A: Compared to the_____ model, the quality is much better. Different colors are available.

B: I'd like to bring up the topic of packaging. Please state your _____ about packaging.

A: All right, as you know, packaging has a close bearing on sales. We hope that the new packaging will _____ our clients.

B: Yes, it also _____ the reputation of the products. How are the candles packed? I'm afraid the cardboard boxes are not strong enough for ocean transportation.

A: They're packed in strong _____ boxes. How do you prefer the goods to be dispatched, by rail or by sea?

B: By sea. Because of the high cost of railway _____, we prefer sea transportation.

A: I agree with you.

B: When can you guarantee shipment? I'm terribly _____ about late shipment.

A: We can guarantee shipment in December or early next year at the very _____.

B: That's fine.

IV. Role Play

Work in pairs or more. Try to act out the following situation.

Suppose you work as a receptionist at your display in Mobile Apps and Game Development Company. A client is interested in your products. Try to introduce your products to him.

V. Writing and Speaking

Write one sentence on your own for each of the following words or expressions and speak them out to your partner. Then your partner interprets them into Chinese.

1. display area

2. superior quality

3. competitive price

4. detailed description

5. ready market

6. quality control department

会展之窗
The Window of the Convention & Exhibition

How to Make a Good Sales Introduction

Making a sales introduction can be nerve-wracking. Throw in a recession and increased pressure to close the sale, and the scenario gets even more stressful. Generic speeches and snazzy PowerPoint slides just don't cut it anymore — especially with corporate customers who have reduced spending to boost their bottom lines. That's why firms like IBM have retooled their sales pitches to better address the needs of their customers. Before setting up your next meeting with a potential client, try these techniques to create a more effective sales presentation that can produce real results.

Know Their Pain

Goal: Target your sales pitch to address the problems your customers need to solve.

There are no one-size-fits-all solutions when it comes to framing a sales pitch. Even within the same industry, each potential customer will have a unique set of problems that he is eager to address. Your job is to understand those needs and position your pitch to speak directly to the client's core concerns.

To do this effectively, good research is essential. The customer's website is a good place to begin, but keep digging deeper. "Prospective clients expect that you understand their business, because websites, social networking, and other forms of technology are accessible to everyone," says Kyla O'Connell, a sales consultant and director of business development for advertising agency punch. "It's not wise to walk in and ask, 'What is the company's vision?' They expect you to know that already." Research the company and its competitors online, but don't stop there.

The Internet is useful, but nothing beats the insight you'll get by talking to a human. That's why it's invaluable to find a contact inside the target company who can advise you. Leverage your social networks or professional organizations to find an "inside coach" who can provide details about what happens behind the closed doors — especially whatever "pain" or existential concerns the firm is confronting.

Lastly, try to learn as much as possible about the person who will make the purchasing decision. The buyer may be under intense pressure to solve a problem, or face losing her job. Once you have a handle on what that problem is, your presentation should position your products or services as a solution. Potential customers are always more receptive when it's clear that the sales pitch is relevant to their circumstances.

Big Idea

Studying the industry as much as the players getting to know the inner workings of a company — and its decision makers — is a crucial part of any effective sales pitch. But don't miss the bigger picture: what's happening in the industry. Keep up with the trade magazines, seminars, newsletters, conventions, or online groups that provide insight into an industry.

In 2001, IBM executives asked their customers what IBM sales reps lacked. The answer, according to an interview in *Sales and Marketing Management Magazine*, was that IBM's sales force did not have sufficient depth of knowledge about the customers' industries. To address this, IBM retrained its sales force to make each sales rep an industry expert. Reps were also reorganized into teams based on a customer's size, industry, and location. The shift meant that all of IBM's sales reps could respond quickly to their customers' needs — without having to defer to a superior or another employee with specialized industry knowledge.

Design a Sales Introduction that Sings — Not Snoozes

Goal: Create an engaging pitch targeted to your potential customer.

Resist the urge to cobble together a bunch of pre-existing PowerPoint slides, and instead try to create a presentation that tells a clear story with a beginning, a middle, and an end. Dean Brenner of the Latimer Group, a communications consulting firm, urges salespeople to sit down and outline the story they want to tell before writing the final draft. Begin by setting a goal, he says. Consider these two questions: What do I want to accomplish? What do I want my customers to think when I finish the presentation? If a competitor sells a cheaper product, then "your goal is to get them to see value beyond the price," Brenner says. "All communication needs to be constructed with a very clear picture of where you're trying to go."

Clarify your message before pulling in props such as PowerPoint slides, brochures, or decks. "Those things are merely the final illustration of the story you're trying to tell," Brenner says. Showing a picture, video, or graphic to illustrate a point is fine, but avoid showing a series of slides that contain nothing but text. "Too many salespeople use PowerPoint slides as a crutch and simply read the slides to the audience," O'Connell adds. Most importantly, avoid what O'Connell calls the "shameful rookie mistake" of turning a sales presentation into a dog-and-pony show that describes how great your company is — but doesn't address your potential customers' problems.

Checklist

Develop an introduction.

Before you head into the meeting, make sure you have all your ducks in a row. Here are a few things you won't want to forget:

Determine the points you want to make which are tailored to the specific customers.

Write out your goals for the meeting.

Take your insights into your customers' needs and turn them into a story with a solid beginning, middle, and end.

Create the visual aids that best illustrate the story.

Eliminate jargon and confusing slides from the introduction.

Practice, practice, practice.

Get feedback from at least one other source, like your sales coach or a trusted colleague, before the presentation.

Article Source:

http://wenku.baidu.com/view/edab60d726fff705cc170a8a.html

Unit Fifteen

展品物流与运输
Exhibits Logistics & Transportation

Teaching Targets 教学目标

- To learn what exhibits logistics & transportation are
- To learn about the modes of exhibits logistics & transportation
- To master some useful expressions and sentences
- To hold conversations concerning this topic

背景知识
Background Knowledge

　　展品物流是指通过优化资源配置，实现展品的快速、高效流动，降低物流成本，提高服务水平。展品物流不仅包括展品的位移，还包括展品的包装、保管、装卸、流通加工等多方面的内容，物流管理的目标是降低成本、提高效率、加强服务。

　　展品运输是指展品包装结束后，通过运输工具将展品移动至目的地的行为(包括展品装卸作业)。展品运输的责任范围为自出发地的展品包装箱离地时始，至到达目的地的展品包装箱落地时止。

　　从广义上讲，展品运输包括展览前后展品的运输、会展活动期间向参展商和参展观众分发食物的运输，以及与此配套的会展设施的运输等。

　　从狭义上讲，展品运输就是指以展品为主体所产生的运输过程。

热身活动
Warming Up

Listen to the recording carefully and answer the following questions.

1. How many modes of transportation in logistics do you know?

2. How can we choose the modes of transportation?

3. What mode of transportation is usually used to transport bulk products?

4. What kind of products are transported by trucks usually?

5. What are the advantages and disadvantages of air freight?

示范对话
Model Dialogues

Dialogue 1

J=John, an exhibitor; W=Mr. Wu, a staff member of a logistics company

J : Mr. Wu, I'm here to discuss the storage and logistics of our exhibits.

W: You are welcome, John. We are happy to serve you.

J: Our exhibits are delivered to California this time. It's a very long distance. We hope you will pay particular attention to the instructions marked on the wooden cases for storage and delivery.

W: We will.

J: As the goods are fragile, we hope you handle with care.

W: OK. I will ask our warehouse staff to pay extra care of the goods.

J: That would be good! By the way, which type of container do you think is best for our exhibits?

W: A 20-foot container is OK.

J: We will take your advice. What is more, in fact, I have emailed you about it.

W: You mean about the advanced shipment?

J: Yes. We request advanced shipment. At the beginning, we required the exhibits to arrive in California by June 9th. But now, we hope to advance it to June 8th. We want to set up our booth in advance.

W: We have tried to arrange an advanced shipment for your order but regret to tell you that we are not able to comply with your full request.

J: What a pity! What shall we do then?

W: The best thing we can do is to arrange an advanced shipment for 500 pieces on June 8th. The remaining 500 pieces will be dispatched on June 9. Is it all right?

J: Is there any other choice?

W: Sorry. We have tried our utmost after all.

J: OK! We will take your suggestion. We agree to partial shipment.

W: Thank you for your consideration, John.

Word bank

storage ['stɔːrɪdʒ] *n.* 存储；仓库；贮藏所

logistics [lə'dʒɪstɪks] *n.* 物流

deliver [dɪ'lɪvə] *v.* 递送；交付

instruction [ɪn'strʌkʃ(ə)n] *n.* 指令，命令；指示

fragile ['frædʒaɪl] *adj.* 脆的；易碎的

warehouse ['weəhaʊs] *n.* 仓库；货栈

container [kən'teɪnə] *n.* 集装箱

comply [kəm'plaɪ] *v.* 遵守；顺从，遵从

dispatch [dɪ'spætʃ] *v.* 派遣；分派 *n.* 派遣；急件

Notes

1. Mr. Wu, I'm here to discuss the storage and logistics of our exhibits.

吴先生，我来此是想讨论展品的存储和物流。

2. We hope you will pay particular attention to the instructions marked on the wooden cases for storage and delivery.

我们希望您们能够特别注意木箱上标记的存储和交付说明。

3. As the goods are fragile, we hope you handle with care.

由于货物易碎，我们希望您们能够小心轻放。

4. Which type of container do you think is best for our exhibits?

您认为哪种型号的集装箱最适合我们的展品？

5. We have tried to arrange an advanced shipment for your order but regret to tell you that we are not able to comply with your full request.

我们已经尽力为贵方的订单安排提前装运，但是很遗憾地告诉您，我们不能完全遵守贵方的要求。

Dialogue 2

Linda(i.e. L) is complaining about the damage of the exhibits and claiming it with Mr. Feng(i.e. F).

L: Mr. Feng, I am here to complain about the damage to our exhibits in transportation.

F: What's the matter?

L: We accepted your partial shipment suggestion, and expected to receive the remaining goods on June 9th. However, we found some of the exhibits were damaged when we received them. Do you know how much it has influenced our exhibition?

F: Linda, we are terribly sorry for the damage. I have checked it, and found that the damage was not under our control because of the vessel's problem. Anyway, we apologize for the damage and hope you understand our constraints.

L: We understand your constraints, but who is responsible for the losses caused by the damage?

F: We will apply for the claims from the insurance company. You know, according to our usual practice. All goods we delivered are insured AAR by China's Insurance Company.

L: OK, I see.

F: But we need your claim information.

L: What claim information do we need to offer?

F: Please prepare the packing list with details of the damaged items. The representative from the insurance company will contact you and arrange to estimate your losses.

L: OK, I understand. We will send it to you tomorrow.

F: I am very sorry for the damage, Ms. Linda.

L: Frankly speaking, we were a little afraid it would destroy our exhibition when we found the problem. Fortunately, our staff finally solved the problem.

F: We hope that would not affect our future relations.

L: It is OK. We understand.

F: Thank you for your consideration. We look forward to your future orders.

L: You are welcome.

Word bank

complain [kəmˈpleɪn] v. 投诉；发牢骚；诉说

claim [kleɪm] v. 要求；声称 n. 索赔，索要

damage [ˈdæmɪdʒ] n. 损害；损毁 v. 损害，毁坏

vessel [ˈves(ə)l] n. 船；舰

constraint [kənˈstreɪnt] n. 约束

estimate [ˈestɪmeɪt] v. 估计；估价

destroy [dɪˈstrɔɪ] v. 破坏；消灭；毁坏

affect [əˈfekt] v. 影响

Notes

1. Mr. Feng, I am here to complain about the damage to our exhibits in transportation.
   冯先生，我来是想就我们展品在运输途中的损坏问题进行投诉。

2. We accepted your partial shipment suggestion, and expected to receive the remaining goods on June 9th.
   我们接受贵方分批装运的建议，并且希望在6月9日收到其余的货物。

3. I have checked it, and found that the damage was not under our control because of

the vessel's problem.

我已经检查过，并发现由于船只的问题导致的损坏并不在我们的控制范围内。

4. We can understand your constraint, but who is responsible for the losses caused by the damage?

我们能够理解贵方的约束条件，但是谁应为损坏造成的损失承担责任呢？

5. You know, according to our usual practice, all goods we delivered are insured AAR by China's Insurance Company.

您知道，根据我们的惯例，我们交付的所有产品都投保了中国保险公司的一切险。

实用句型
Practical Sentence Patterns

1 As the goods are fragile, we hope you handle with care. 由于货物是易碎品，我们希望您们小心轻放。

2 We will take your advice. 我们将接受您的建议。

3 We have tried our utmost after all. 毕竟我们已经尽力了。

4 Thank you for your kind consideration. 谢谢您的关照。

5 I have found that the damage was not under our control because of the vessel's problem. 我发现此次损坏并非我们所能掌控的，因为问题出在船只上。

6 Anyway, we apologize for the damage and hope you understand our constraints. 不过，我们还是为这次的损坏表示抱歉，希望贵公司能体谅我们的局限。

7 We will apply for the claims from the insurance company. 我们将为您们向保险公司申请赔偿。

8 We need your claim information. 我们需要您们提供一些索赔资料。

9 Please prepare the packing list with details of the damaged items. 请准备清单，详列所有损毁物品。

10 The representative from the insurance company will contact you and arrange to estimate your losses. 保险公司代表将与贵公司联系，评估您们的损失。

11 Thank you for your consideration. We look forward to your future orders. 非常感谢您的理解。我们期待您今后的订单。

12 How long does it usually take you to make a delivery? 通常您们需要多长时间交货？

⑬ Could you possibly advance shipment further more? 您们能不能再提前一点发货？

⑭ We'll try our best to advance shipment to June. 我们会尽最大努力将发货时间提前到六月。

⑮ When is the earliest possible date you can ship the goods? 您们最早什么时候可以装运？

⑯ I wonder whether you can make shipment in July. 我想知道您们能否在七月份装运。

⑰ How long will the delivery take from here to America by sea freight? 从这里到美国海运需要多长时间？

⑱ We will contact the factory and see if they can manage to advance delivery by a month. 我们将联系工厂，看一下他们能否提前一个月装运。

实践实训项目
Practical Training Project

I. Building Up Your Vocabulary

1. Match the words on the left with the best translations on the right.

(1) transportation	a. 派遣
(2) logistics	b. 运输
(3) shipment	c. 物流
(4) deliver	d. 仓库
(5) storage	e. 保险
(6) container	f. 索赔
(7) claim	g. 集装箱
(8) insurance	h. 存储
(9) warehouse	i. 发货
(10) dispatch	j. 装运

2. Complete the following dialogue with proper words or expressions.

A= a staff member of a logistics company; B=a customer of the company

B: I am happy we have settled _____(支付条款). When is the earliest shipment you can make?

A: It usually takes us one month to delivery. You know we should get the goods ready, make out the documents, and _____(预订舱位).

B: When is the exact _____(发货时间)?

A: We can make prompt shipment _____(五月底).

B: _____(恐怕) the date of shipment would be late for us.

A: The manufacturers are fully committed. They have no stock on hand.

B: But _____(即期装运) is of great importance for us.

A: I see.

B: After the arrival of the shipment, the flow of the goods through the _____(营销渠道) takes at least three weeks before the goods can reach us.

A: Well. We will contact the factory and see if they can manage to_____(提前交货) by a month.

B: That would be fine.

A: How about _____(部分装运)? We can ship whatever is ready to meet your urgent need instead of waiting for the whole lot to get ready.

B: We will consider your suggestion.

A: Another problem is _____(舱位). Even if we had the goods ready, I do not think we could ship them in February.

B: I know there is a _____(大量的需求) on shipping lately.

A: Anyhow we will try our best to _____(满足您的需求).

B: In case you should fail to effect delivery within the stipulated time, we should have to declare a claim against you for the loss and reserve the right to _____(撤销合同).

B: We know that. I assure you the shipment will be effected _____(及时).

A: Thank you for your cooperation.

B: You are welcome.

II. Substitution Drills

Replace the underlined words with the words in the following boxes.

1. These shipping tips will help you ship quickly and <u>efficiently</u> so that you can provide your buyers with a great experience.

with efficiency	expeditiously	effectively

2. Pack your item for shipment after you take pictures — but before you list — so you can have <u>accurate</u> package weight and dimensions to include during the listing process.

exact	precise	right	proper

3. Make sure your item arrives safely by packing it securely. Use a sturdy box that's the right size, make sure to include enough packing material, and tape it <u>securely</u>.

> safely   firmly   without damage

4. Buyers <u>typically</u> want their items quickly, so the faster you can get your items shipped, the happier your buyers will be.

> usually   commonly   generally

5. <u>Consider</u> offering either same business day or 1 business day handling, and tell your buyer when an item is shipped.

> think about   take account of   reckon

6. By <u>meeting</u> certain shipping conditions, you can automatically receive 5-star detailed seller rating for shipping time.

> satisfying   reaching   obtaining

7. If you sell <u>valuable</u> items, consider purchasing shipping insurance. Check with your shipping carrier for insurance options.

> precious   rare   worthy   priceless

8. You can print shipping <u>labels</u> and custom forms right from your home printer.

> tags   marks   descriptions

9. Every <u>firm</u> requires the movement of goods from a point to another point.

> company   enterprise   business

10. Transportation refers to the physical movement of goods from a point of <u>origin</u> to a point of consumption.

> start   beginning   source

III. Listening Comprehension

Listen to the dialogue and fill in the blanks according to what you hear. Then practice the dialogue with your partner.

A= a staff member of a global logistics group; B=a client of the group

A: Speaking of your order, No. 168, I'm afraid we can't ship _____ at one time.

B: Is there anything wrong with my order?

A: As far as your order is concerned, everything is all right. Only it's difficult for us to get so many exhibits prepared within _____ .

B: What are your suggestions?

A: I propose that _____ be allowed.

B: But the exhibition will be held _____. So it will be better to ship them all at once.

A: Maybe you are not clear about _____ yet. It is in your own interests that we put forward such a proposal. If a partial shipment is allowed, instead of waiting for the whole lot to _____, we can ship whatever is ready to meet your _____.

B: Oh, I see. _____ I agree to partial shipment. Please by all means guarantee the date of shipment so that we wouldn't miss the _____.

A: We can assure you that the shipment of your order will be effected in May at the latest. There is _____.

B: By the way, we do hope you can make a _____.

A: We'll try our best. In case there is no direct shipment, will you consider allowing transshipment?

B: I'm afraid not. You know, transshipment takes _____. What's more, there are risks of damage to the exhibits during transshipment. I hope you will try some other way.

A: How about this then? I'll contact the _____ again and ask them to make delivery a week in advance.

B: That's _____! Thanks a lot!

A: You are welcome.

IV. Role Play

Work in pairs or more. Try to act out the following situation.

Suppose you are working for a company which is going to participate in an exhibition abroad. You are negotiating with a manager of a logistics company about the storage and transportation of the exhibits.

V. Writing and Speaking

Write one sentence on your own for each of the following words or expressions and speak them out to your partner. Then your partner interprets them into Chinese.

1. storage and logistics

2. handle with care

3. usual practice

4. claim information

5. packing list

6. future orders

7. make delivery

8. advance shipment

会展之窗
The Window of the Convention & Exhibition

Tips for Successful Shipping

These shipping tips will help you ship quickly and efficiently so that you can provide your buyers with a great eBay experience.

Know your shipping charges

Pack your item for shipment after you take pictures — but before you list — so you can have accurate package weight and dimensions to include during the listing process.

Package your items carefully

Make sure your item arrives safely by packing it securely. Use a sturdy box that's the right size, make sure to include enough packing material, and tape it securely. Find out more about packaging items.

Ship quickly

Buyers typically want their items quickly, so the faster you can get your items shipped, the happier your buyers will be. Consider offering either same business day or 1 business day handling, and tell your buyer when an item is shipped.

Tip: By meeting certain shipping conditions, you can automatically receive 5-star detailed seller rating for shipping time.

Save time and hassle on package pickup and insurance

Save time with free package pickup from the U.S. Postal Service. If you sell valuable items, consider purchasing shipping insurance. Check with your shipping carrier for insurance options. You can also purchase shipping insurance when you create and print shipping labels on eBay.

Remember, you can include the cost of insurance in the item's price or handling cost, but you can't charge a separate fee for insurance.

Stock up on supplies

Always have shipping supplies on hand by ordering free eBay U.S. Postal Service supplies, or find shipping supplies from sellers on eBay.

You can also reuse shipping supplies like bubble wrap, packing nuts, and lightly-used cardboard boxes.

Print shipping labels at home

You can print shipping labels and custom forms right from your home printer. Look for the "Print Shipping Label" link in the listing or on the "Order details" page. Learn more about creating and printing your own shipping labels.

Provide tracking information

USPS Tracking is included at no extra charge when you create and print a shipping label on eBay. You can also upload your own tracking or delivery confirmation information in "My eBay".

Please remember that in order to be covered by the eBay Money Back Guarantee, we do require signature confirmation for those packages valued at more than $750. If your transaction is $750 or more, signature confirmation will be preselected for you. You can remove this option, however, requiring a signature at delivery helps protect you if your buyer doesn't receive the item and opens a case.

Generate repeat business

Include a business card or note with your eBay user ID to thank your buyer for their business.

Article Source:

http://pages.ebay.com/help/pay/shipping-tips.html

Unit `Sixteen`

展会风险管理

Exhibition Risk Management

Teaching Targets 教学目标

- To learn about what risk management is
- To learn to cope with contingencies
- To master some words and expressions related to contingencies
- To master some words and expressions related to exhibit insurance
- To hold conversations concerning this topic

背景知识
Background Knowledge

即便是精心策划和熟练操办的展会也可能会因突发事件而影响正常秩序。突发事件考验了展会承办商及展会服务经理的魄力和领导力。

展会服务经理须制订全面的事故应急计划，涵盖火灾、盗窃、炸弹威胁及不可抗力灾害等突发事件，计划应包括以下三方面内容：描述可能发生的情形；概括每种情形的应急程序；明确列出执行各项任务的责任人。

热身活动
Warming Up

Listen to the recording carefully and answer the following questions.

1. What can a risk be defined as?

2. What is risk management?

3. What's the purpose of risk management?

4. Why is public opinion so important to an organization?

5. What are the results of bad employees in a company?

示范对话
Model Dialogues

Dialogue 1

Ada(i.e. A), an exhibition service manager, is talking with Peter(i.e. P), an exhibitor, about how to maintain the safety and cope with contingencies during a jewellery show.

P: Good morning, Ada. I'd like to talk to you about the safety issue during the show. You know, as a well-known jewellery brand in China, each piece of our jewellery is very valuable. So, I'm concerned about your security measures.

A: I understand. We've already fixed micro-cameras in every corner of the exhibition halls, providing 24-hour monitor services.

P: I know. I've already checked the site and the video, and found a problem. In the video, a pillar is right in the back of our booth and covers some part of our counter. So, some of our products cannot be seen in the video. Please look at this.

A: Oh, yes. But, have you checked the videos from the other cameras? I believe this covered part can be seen in the other videos, because our engineers are experienced and have not made such a mistake before.

P: OK. Please have a thorough check and make some adjustments if needed.

A: Yes, of course. It's our responsibility. At this show, we apply a new electronic security lock. This type of electronic security lock is physically attached to the exhibits and works in tandem with a sensor.

P: Good.

A: Moreover, we provide you with a brochure with the names and telephone numbers of emergency treatment centers and ambulance firms.

P: You are thoughtful.

A: If you have any questions, please feel free to contact me.

P: OK. Thank you for your work, Ada.

Word bank

maintain [meɪn'teɪn; mən'teɪn] *v.* 维持

contingency [kən'tɪndʒ(ə)nsɪ] *n.* 偶然性；[安全] 意外事故

issue['ɪʃuː; 'ɪsjuː] *n.* 问题

security [sɪ'kjʊərətɪ] *n.* 安全；保证

video ['vɪdɪəʊ] *n.* 视频；录像

thorough ['θʌrə] *adj.* 彻底的

adjustment [ə'dʒʌs(t)m(ə)nt] *n.* 调整，调节

attach [ə'tætʃ] *v.* 使依附；贴上

tandem ['tændəm] *n.* 串联 *adj.* 串联的 *adv.* 一前一后地；纵排地

emergency [ɪ'mɜːdʒ(ə)nsɪ] *n.* 紧急情况；突发事件

ambulance ['æmbjʊl(ə)ns] *n.* 救护车

Notes

1. I'd like to talk to you about the safety issue during the show.

我想与您讨论一下展会期间的安全问题。

2. We've already fixed micro-cameras in every corner of the exhibition halls, providing 24-hour monitor services.

我们已经在展会大厅的每个角落安装了微型摄像机，提供24小时监控服务。

3. In the video, a pillar is right in the back of our booth and covers some part of our counter.

在视频录像中，一根柱子正好在我们展位后面，挡住了我们展台的一部分。

4. I believe this covered part can be seen in other videos, because our engineers are experienced and have not made such a mistake before.

我相信这个被遮挡的部分可以在其他视频录像中看到，因为我们的工程师很有经验，以前从来没有犯过这样的错误。

5. This type of electronic security lock is physically attached to the exhibits and works in tandem with a sensor.

这种电子安全锁实际地贴附在展品上并与传感器串联工作。

Dialogue 2

A=organizer; B=exhibitor

A: Cindy, we are very sorry to inform you that the time of the Global Organic Food & Beverage Exposition which you had decided to attend would be changed due to the organizer.

B: Please give us an explanation.

A: We were very shocked to hear that news just now. Because a temporary meeting will be held there, it would be postponed for 10 days.

B: You really get our goat.

A: We are really sorry for that. We will deduct 3,000 Yuan for your participation fee, which will return to you during the show. If you want to withdraw, we can return all the fees back to you at once.

B: OK, we will consider it carefully.

A: Cindy, you can visit the comprehensive exhibition which I talked to you about before. If you'd like to participate in that exhibition, I can send you the invitation letters, and then you can take part in that exhibition.

B: Is this free or not?

A: Only the academic forum during the exhibition is free, but if you still want to participate in the delayed exhibition, we can compensate you for the exhibition. What do you think about this?

B: OK, we will consider your advice carefully.

Word bank

exposition [ekspə'zɪʃ(ə)n] *n.* 博览会；展览会

destine ['destɪn] *v.* 注定；命定；预定

temporary ['temp(ə)rərɪ] *adj.* 暂时的，临时的

postpone [pəʊs(t)'pəʊn; pə'spəʊn] *v.* 使……延期；延缓，延迟，把……放在后面

decrease [dɪ'kriːs] *n.* 减少，减小；减少量 *v.* 减少，减小

withdraw [wɪð'drɔː] *v.* 收回；撤销

comprehensive [kɒmprɪ'hensɪv] *adj.* 综合的；广泛的

academic [ækə'demɪk] *adj.* 学术的

forum ['fɔːrəm] *n.* 论坛，讨论会

compensate ['kɒmpenseɪt] *v.* 补偿，赔偿；抵消

Notes

1. Cindy, we are very sorry to inform you that the time of the Global Organic Food & Beverage Exposition which you had destined should be changed for some reasons of the organizer.

辛迪，我很遗憾地通知您，由于主办方的原因，您预定参加的全球有机食品饮品博览会的时间将有些变化。

2. We were very shocked to hear that news just now. Because a temporary meeting will be held there, it would be postponed for 10 days.

我们刚刚听到这个消息时也很震惊，因为有一个临时的会议要在那里举行，所以展会延期10天。

3. You really get our goat.

这真让我们恼火。

4. We are terribly sorry for that. We will decrease 3,000 Yuan for your participation fee, which will return to you during the show.

我们为此深感抱歉，我们会将您的参展费用减低3000元，并在展会期间将这笔钱返还给您。

5. If you'd like to participate in that exhibition, I can send you the invitation letters, and then you can take part in that exhibition.

如果您想参加那个展会，我可以寄送邀请信给您，然后您可以参加那个展会。

实用句型
Practical Sentence Patterns

1 Our company cannot participate in this exhibition for our schedule has been changed with the reason of three VIP clients will visit our company. 我们公司的日程表有些变化，不能按时参展了，因为届时我们有三个VIP客户要招待。

2 We have reported your company's name into the organizing committee. 贵公司的名称已经上报给组委会了。

3 Would you like to take part in another exhibition? 您会考虑参加另外一个展会吗?

4 We have the name list of the participants from the international companies. 我这边有来自全球企业的参展商名单。

5 It must be the best way for us if the exhibition does not conflict with our time. 如果该展会和我们的时间不冲突，那就再好不过了。

6 We are very sorry to inform you that your place has been moved into place B. 我们很抱歉地通知您，您们的展位被移到B馆了。

7 Because the organizer wants to distribute all the participants with qualification, they have to modify the place. 因为现在组委会决定将参展商都按照限制条件统一分配，所以展位需要调整。

8 Shall we get the information about the layout of the exhibition now? 我们能了解一下目前这个展会的布置情况吗?

9 Is there any influence about the change, such as is it well-known among the participants? 这样的改变会不会有什么影响? 比如说参展商都知道吗?

10 You'd better choose one as soon as you can for the layout came out just now, so you have many choices. 因为展位布置图刚刚出来，所以最好尽快确定，这样能有比较宽松的选择余地。

⑪ I've already checked the site and the video, and found a problem. 我已经检查了我们的场地和视频，发现了一个问题。

⑫ Have you checked the videos from the other cameras? 您检查过其他摄像机的视频吗？

⑬ Please have a thorough check and do some adjustment if needed. 请进行一次彻底的检查，如果需要的话，做一些调整。

⑭ If you have any questions, please feel free to contact me. 如果您有什么问题，请随时联系我。

实践实训项目
Practical Training Project

I. Building Up Your Vocabulary

1. Match the words on the left with the best translations on the right.

(1) risk	a. 主办方
(2) emergency	b. 补偿
(3) issue	c. 撤回
(4) security	d. 拖延
(5) thorough	e. 调整
(6) adjustment	f. 彻底的
(7) postpone	g. 安全
(8) withdraw	h. 问题
(9) compensate	i. 突发事件
(10) organizer	j. 风险

2. Complete the following dialogue with proper words or expressions.

A: Excuse me, can we change _____(布局) for we want a much larger place?

B: Please wait a moment and I will _____(查看数据库). Your place is B-3 with 18 square meters, but how large of the place would you prefer?

A: How about 36 _____(平方米)?

B: All the places have been booked, but here is a place of 32 square meters which the participant think _____(稍微大了些) for them. Would you like to change your place with them?

A: Is there any other choice? We'd like to bring two machines there, so we are afraid that the place would not be ＿＿＿＿＿(足够大) for us.

B: If so, we will help you to check if there is anyone who ＿＿＿＿＿(撤出) from the exhibition or apply for a larger one to the organizer.

A: Which method would be faster?

B: It is possible for some clients, who may withdraw from the exhibition, but it needs to meet chances. We are more sure of applying a new place to the organizer, but the new one might be ＿＿＿＿＿(稍微远点儿) from the national hall or the organizer may arrange the new place in other countries' place.

A: That's OK, but ＿＿＿＿＿(样式与标识) should be in line with the country, am I right?

B: Yes, same style. The only question is the distance, and if you decide to do this, we should ＿＿＿＿＿(向组办方申请) as soon as possible.

A: OK, I will tell my boss and inform you once we ＿＿＿＿＿(做出决定).

II. Substitution Drills

Replace the underlined words with the words in the following boxes.

1. Consider the benefits and <u>risks</u> to your business when deciding to exhibit your products or services.

dangers hazards harms

2. These will be different for each event; however, there can be a lot to <u>gain</u> from promoting your products in person within a different environment.

get obtain achieve

3. Exhibitions are open to a large and sometimes <u>diverse</u> range of audience (usually the general public).

different various dissimilar

4. This provides you with a platform to promote your products or services to a <u>broader</u> group that may have little or no knowledge of your products or services.

larger wider extended

5. Depending on your type of business, product and market testing can be carried out at exhibitions to gain industry or general <u>opinion</u> about your offering.

view idea statement

6. Being involved in an exhibition can provide you with opportunities to branch out to business-to-business trading and <u>create</u> a customer database from the visitors to your display booth.

produce set up establish

7. It is also important to ensure that you have <u>thoroughly</u> researched before attending an exhibition, and if you have any business advisers, discuss it with them.

> entirely   completely   totally   fully

8. There will probably be quite a bit of <u>competition</u> at all shows.

> challenge   match   rat race   ferocity

9. Choosing the wrong exhibition to exhibit your business's products or services can <u>result in</u> displaying to the wrong audience.

> lead to   bring about   give rise to

10. Poor promotion can mean the costs of attending the exhibition outweigh any <u>revenue</u> you gain.

> income   returns   profit   earnings

III. Listening Comprehension

Listen to the dialogue and fill in the blanks according to what you hear. Then practice the dialogue with your partner.

A: Bad news! The consignment of our exhibition items arrived at the destination is nonfunctional. We have to _____.

B: That really _____! Did you have them insured?

A: Yes. We were insured for _____ because I thought of it. We would be covered for everything.

B: Don't put all your eggs in one basket. It is true that "All Risks" is of the broadest kind of _____, but it does not really cover all risks. For example, the "All Risks" excludes coverage against the damage caused by war, strikes, and riots. What is the cause for the _____ do you think?

A: I think the damage was due to _____.

B: Oh, then I am afraid the _____ would refuse to pay for the damage thus caused.

A: Why?

B: Obviously, because it is the shipping company that contributes to the loss through _____. The responsibility should rest with it. Don't you think so?

A: Well, thank you very much for all your _____. And now I am sure what I should do next.

IV. Role Play

Work in pairs or more. Try to act out the following situation.

Suppose you are working for a Jewellery Company which is going to participate in an

International Jewellery Exposition. You are discussing with a service manager of the exhibition center about the security issues.

V. Writing and Speaking

Write one sentence on your own for each of the following words or expressions and speak them out to your partner. Then your partner interprets them into Chinese.

1. the layout of the exhibition
2. well-known
3. safety issue
4. micro-camera
5. monitor services
6. thorough check

会展之窗
The Window of the Convention & Exhibition

Planning an Event? Better Have a Contingency Plan

Event planning is a difficult process, whether you're a layperson or a public relations pro. Schedules need to be coordinated, collateral material needs to be assembled, and presentations need to be prepared. Entertainment and catering services may need to be booked, and guests must be attended to. Securing a site for an event can prove troublesome depending on the budget, and setting an agenda can be a pain when too many people are involved in the planning process. But as I learned recently, sometimes the biggest secret to successful event planning is having a contingency plan.

The weather was great in the Berkshires. I was in the mountains of western Massachusetts to celebrate the wedding of a good friend, and the guests marveled at the good fortune bestowed on us by Mother Nature.

"If only the weather was like this last week," one guest muttered to me.

Probing, I found out that this guest had helped plan a public event to launch a new product by a company based in upstate New York, just a few hours from where we enjoyed the wedding festivities. The event took place outdoors, which would have been fine had it not poured rain.

"We had no contingency plan," the guest, an executive at the company, told me. "The people who planned it banked on good weather, and when it started to rain, we had to rush everyone into the cafeteria."

"Journalists, business partners, and employees crowded into the cafeteria," the guest said, "because it was the only room in the office complex large enough to handle the crowd."

"It was a disaster," the guest continued, asking me not to reveal his company's name for fear of additional embarrassment. "We had to spend more than 30 minutes setting up the sound system so people could hear us and the acoustics in the cafeteria proved to be horrible."

The rest of the event did not go much better and people's moods soured due to the poor sound and the flustered presentations. Media coverage of the event, which the company hoped would be the catalyst for a public relations campaign, was minuscule.

"We had a wire reporter there and we were hoping that his story would make it onto the national wire," said the executive. "He couldn't hear the presentation though, so he never wrote about it."

I asked the executive who was to blame and he smiled: "The public relations people, of course. They planned it."

Preparing a contingency plan is a must when it comes to effective event planning. As the example above illustrates, weather can have an obvious impact on an event planned to take place outdoors. In this particular case, the people planning the event should have prepared the cafeteria ahead of time and shifted the event indoors once the morning weather report hit. Even a "chance of showers" can ruin an event.

I did ask the executive one more question about the event.

"Had the public relations department ever planned such an event before?" I asked.

"No," he replied. "This was the first time we ever did something like this."

"Lesson learned," I said, as we toasted to the happy couple.

Article Source:

http://www.ereleases.com/prfuel/planning-an-event-better-have-a-contingency-plan/

参考文献

[1] 崔益红. 会展概论[M]. 2版. 北京：北京大学出版社，2015.

[2] 徐静，高跃. 会展概论[M]. 2版. 北京：北京大学出版社，2017.

[3] 李世平，于海波. 会展情景英语[M]. 长春：东北师范大学出版社，2019.

[4] 张占军. 会展英语[M]. 北京：中国商务出版社，2010.

[5] 吴云. 会展交际英语[M]. 上海: 立信会计出版社，2004.

[6] 张占军，张宝敏. 会展英语[M]. 北京: 中国商务出版社，2005.

[7] 卢思源. 会展英语[M]. 上海: 上海科学技术文献出版社，2005.

[8] 朱学宁，杨国民，舒立志. 会展实务英语教程[M]. 北京：北京师范大学出版社，2011.

[9] 邱玉华. 实用会展英语[M]. 北京：北京大学出版社，2009.

[10] 桑龙扬，杜清萍. 实用商务旅行与会展英语[M]. 北京：机械工业出版社，2010.

[11] 吴云. 会展实用英语(读写篇) [M]. 北京：旅游教育出版社，2007.

[12] 李红英. 会展英语实用教程[M]. 大连：大连理工大学出版社，2008.

[13] 宿荣江，曹珊珊，周媛. 会展实用英语[M]. 北京：中国人民大学出版社，2008.

[14] 沈金辉. 会展实用英语[M]. 北京：机械工业出版社，2012.

[15] 蓝星，冯修文. 会展实务英语·口语[M]. 上海：上海交通大学出版社，2009.

[16] 胡志勇. 会展英语[M]. 上海：上海科学技术文献出版社，2009.

[17] 李世平，黄彬. 会展英语[M]. 北京: 北京大学出版社，2013.

[18] 黄建凤. 会展英语现场口译[M]. 武汉：武汉大学出版社，2010.

[19] 李洪涛，马恒芬. 会展商贸英语实用教程[M]. 天津：天津出版传媒集团，2013.

[20] 孟广君，王栩彬. 会展英语教程[M]. 北京：对外经贸大学出版社，2012.

[21] 盛小利. 一天一场景会展英语[M]. 济南：山东科学技术出版社，2009.

[22] 董元元，迟欢玲. 国际会展英语口语[M]. 大连：大连理工大学出版社，2011.

[23] 张达球，陈宜平，周岩. 会展实务英语[M]. 北京：化学工业出版社， 2008.

[24] 黄晨，柯淑萍. 会展英语[M]. 杭州：浙江大学出版社， 2007.

[25] 蔡龙文，黄冬梅. 会展实务英语[M]. 北京：对外经济贸易大学出版社，2011.

[26] http://www.tceb.or.th/about-us/tceb-intelligence-center/mice-industry.html

[27] http://www.tradeindia.com/about_products/82/Exhibition-Advertising.html

[28] http://www.biztradeshows.com/media-advertising/

[29] http://www.globalnegotiator.com/

[30] http://www.ehow.com/list_6681393_show-booth-design-ideas.html

[31] http://www.businessknowhow.com/marketing/sales-presentation.htm

附录：课文听力材料

Unit 1

How to Prepare for a Meeting

Preparing for a meeting that you have called can be time consuming. You need to first determine the subject of the meeting, who should attend, while also providing a sufficient amount of time for the invited attendees to prepare for the meeting if you expect them to provide their ideas or suggestions. You should also prepare a written agenda, and send it in advance to the meeting attendees. Meetings can last five minutes and still be effective or last hours for a more complex agenda. But the most important is that there's a clearly communicated purpose or agenda, and that the meeting attendees know in advance that they may need to prepare and be actively engaged during the meeting. Your good planning will determine the success of the meeting.

Unit 2

Tips on Picking a Venue for a Meeting

When planning any meeting, venue selection is one of the crucial steps in order for it to be a success.

Choose the Correct Venue for Space and Theme

The first step during this process is: start by making a rough draft of your guest list. You want to make sure that you're looking for venues that have your capacity. You want to eliminate venues that are too big and any that are too small.

Some other key points to have in mind: the concept of the meeting. You want to make sure your venue matches the style and the aesthetics of your meeting.

Consider the Weather

Next, if you are considering a venue within an outdoor space, consider your backup options. Is there going to be rain or inclement weather? Does the venue offer an alternate indoor space? Or can it be tented?

Visit the Meeting Venue and Make Sure It is Appropriate

Schedule a site visit. It's very important to fully review the site in person. Consider for example: where the parking is located, condition of the ballroom, lighting, noise distraction, the distance of the kitchen from the room, and restroom access.

Privacy: ask your venue if they take multiple meetings at the same time. It's always important to make sure that other meetings taking place would not impede in yours.

Unit 3

What Comes Included in Your Hotel Meeting Room?

If you are looking to find a suitable meeting room for your upcoming meeting such as one in a meeting room of Amsterdam city centre, be it for a charity event or for your company, you can look online now to find the best one to suit your needs, but you will probably want to make sure you get the most for your money. This is why it is important that you check exactly what comes with your meeting room when booking it to avoid any hidden charges.

Of course, all hotels offer different features and facilities for their meeting rooms, but you can generally expect many of the same things. For instance, the hotel that you choose should be able to arrange a buffet for everyone attending your meeting so that you can ensure everyone is fed and watered before sitting down to business. They should also be able to provide you with any IT equipment that you will need for your meeting, and could even arrange for transport following it.

Unit 4

The Steps of Registration

Step 1:

Login. If you do not have a personal login, please create one. If you are registering another individual, you must use that individual's login information. Not sure if you have a profile or forgotten how to login? Please use the member password feature or contact Member Services at 888-666-1111.

Not a member? Join today to receive the lowest registration rate.

Step 2:

Please select your registration type and then click "Register Now" to complete your registration: Full Registration.

Step 3:

Register Now.

Step 4:

Complete your registration by going through the checkout. You will not be able to save an incomplete registration to finish at a later time. Within 24 hours of registering, you will receive a receipt and e-mail confirmation. If you do not receive either of these, please contact the registration staff.

Payment Information

All online registration and membership must be prepaid by credit card (Visa, Mastercard, Discover, or American Express).

Unit 5

Conference Room Layout Ideas

Proper space planning is necessary for conducting a successful business meeting. Uncomfortable furniture layout can cause delays in presentations or serve as a distraction to meeting attendees. Plan your conference room layout to suit the size of the group and the activities scheduled to take place during the meeting.

Presenter Style

When you have a designated speaker or presenter for your meeting, you can arrange your tables in the shape of a "U" with the presenter stationed at a podium at the opening in the tables. The base of the "U" shape should be closest to the door where possible, so that the early guests can fill in closest to the speaker, while the late guests can fill in to the seats nearest to the door without causing a disturbance. This layout allows the speaker to interact with the guests and use the floor in the center of the room if he prefers to move about while speaking.

Break-out Meetings

At major conferences and key note addresses, speakers may direct guests to participate in topical break-out sessions. A break-out session consists of a series of small groups discussing assigned topics together. If the participants are seated at one table together, conversations may run together between groups, causing the noise level to rise unnecessarily as the participants struggle to hear the group members. Arrange your tables scattered about the conference room so that the guests can talk comfortably among themselves.

Classroom

The classroom-style conference room layout is suitable for note taking and for meetings requiring multiple handouts or use of tools such as laptop computers. In a classroom layout, rows of narrow conference tables with chairs face the front of a room. Each table provides writing space for each person. This is a comfortable arrangement for long sessions, as refreshments can be placed within reach of each attendee. This setup works best when minimal interaction between the presenter and the audience is expected to take place, such as when the participants are taking a test or studying reference material.

Unit 6

Opening Ceremony Speech

Good morning, everybody!

I'm honored to be here and give my speech to all of you. I could still remember that a year ago I was excitedly standing here and curious about all the things happening in the new campus. At that time, I was wondering how wonderful and comfortable college life would be. You may now have the same idea as mine but what I have to tell you is that college is not only a place to have fun, but also a place to study for yourself, and college life is never so relaxing unless you'd like to fail to get the graduation certificate.

Absolutely, college life is really attractive with numerous kinds of corporations and activities. I believe most of you are eager to take part in different corporations to enjoy yourselves because you were treated like prisoners and devoted to all your subjects in high school. However, here comes a difficult problem for you to make a decision. How do you balance your study and your corporation activities? In fact, I have tried my best to solve the problem but still get nowhere.

To sum up, as your senior, I feel responsible to point out one of the hardest problems you may later come across in your college life and I hope all of you will be able to get well prepared. After all, I hope all of you can have a wonderful time studying and playing in the campus and best wishes to you!

Yours sincerely,

James

Unit 7

Reputation First, Customer Foremost

Good cooking is regarded as an art. Good service is an art, too. But the food and beverage department employees, especially waiters, waitresses, and bartenders, often fail to play the role in creating a good atmosphere. Actually this is the service they sell. High-quality service is dependent on the waiters and the other food and beverage department staff members as well. They should have knowledge of their work right down to the last detail.

The initial contact between the customers and the staff can leave a deep impression. A poor waiter fails to satisfy the requirements of both the customers and the restaurant as well, while a good waiter brings satisfaction to the customers, higher pay to himself, and bigger profits to the restaurant.

In conclusion, good knowledge and skill, a cordial smile, plenty of courtesy with sincere effort and efficiency can certainly cook up a most inviting "dish", a "dish" which will bring into full play the motto "Reputation first, customer foremost".

Unit 8

Meetings and Incentive Travel

Integrating meetings and incentive travel are becoming a more common practice. Companies are taking advantage of the situation when they have their highest performers gathered in one place at the travel destination. They are providing exclusive business content to help their top performers continue to grow and align with the company's business objectives. Successfully incorporating meetings and incentive travel require more than your own experience and intuition. It demands a clear understanding of the preferences of your audience. You have to find the right mix of location, activities and content, meeting format and length, guest policy and rule structure for incentive tours and travel. All of these attributes work together to impact the effectiveness of your meeting and incentive travel reward. Ideally your business objectives will be purposefully woven into everything in your plan.

Unit 9

Types of Exhibitions

An exhibition is an event to collectively display different art, products, or skills. Both individuals and businesses partake in this event to reach specific goals. Various types of exhibitions are especially organized to cater to the needs of the participants.

Exhibitions can be categorized into museums, art exhibitions, trade exhibitions, and consumer exhibitions.

Museums are devoted to conservation of valuable scientific, artistic, cultural, and historical objects. It is open for public viewing which aims to give its visitors significant knowledge. It is a non-commercial type of exhibition since its purpose is to protect its collection from being lost and damaged and make them last for years.

Art exhibitions can include paintings, figurines, drawings, and photos. They can be commercial and non-commercial.

Trade shows are events between organizations and businesses. They are designed to let the participants showcase their products and services and see if it can gain the interest of another company. They are commercial exhibitions but only those invited can attend.

Consumer exhibitions are taken advantage by different companies to expose their products and services to the public. The idea behind this event is to attract the public to buy their products or services.

Unit 10

Benefits of Attending Trade Shows

Consider the benefits to your business when deciding to exhibit your products or services. These will be different for each event; however, there can be a lot to gain from promoting your products in person within a different environment.

Benefits for exhibitors:

※Media exposure for the industry as a whole and for specific companies.

※An opportunity to show the wares to an interested public.

※To find out what is happening in the industry and to evaluate the competitor.

Benefits for visitors:

※The ease of judging relative standards and prices, an opportunity to find out what is happening in the industry, the convenience of everything in one place, and a chance to talk to exhibitors.

Unit 11

Trade Show Planning:
Your Roadmap to Success

Thoughtful, strategic trade show planning is essential to achieving your exhibiting goals and maximizing your return on investment, which includes both your money and time.

The first step in the process is to identify opportunistic conferences and events that reach your target audience of potential buyers.

Start the research process by talking with current customers and learn about the events they attend. Then, contact professional organizations and colleagues in your industry for additional suggestions.

Ensure the show you select draws the type and number of prospects you want. Other considerations include geography, timing, cost, and sponsor reputation.

To promote sales, consider your need for audio-visual rental equipment, sound systems, and mobile technology including iPad and tablet rental. Promotional items, literature, special displays, and other marketing tools should always be included in the consideration mix.

Unit 12

What are the Best Tips for Trade Show Giveaways?

The best tips for trade show giveaways can be divided into two categories, which are choosing the best items and making sure people know about them. Unique promotional items that no other booths have can drive up demand, as can items or devices that are actually useful. Prominent display racks, cases, and signs can help show people that a booth has good trade show giveaways, as can well prepared and outfitted staffers. If efforts are undertaken to ensure that people know about the giveaways at a particular booth, it can result in a marked upsurge in foot traffic. Special events can also be held at the booth during specific times of the day depending on the policies of the particular trade show.

One of the best ways to increase booth traffic is to have some good trade show giveaways, but these items can also help promote a particular message or general brand awareness. Choosing the right items can ensure that people not only stop by a booth but also remember the business later on. If possible, a promotional item should evoke the type of businesses or service rather than being branded merchandise.

Unit 13

Exhibition Invitation Letter

Whenever you are holding an exhibition, it is essential to let people know about it. Exhibition invitation letters are the best way to invite people in the same industry. This letter acts as a personal request to others and is a cordial way to enhance your contracts and business. One should keep in mind that all the essential information regarding the exhibition should be provided, including the date, time, and venue of the event. One should be very attentive while writing this invitation letter to attend an exhibition. There should be no grammatical or spelling errors. Exhibition invitation letters should not be hand written. These letters should be written in a humble tone and should show gratitude. The letter should be clear and concise and there should be no possibility of misunderstanding.

Tips for Writing an Invitation Letter to Attend an Exhibition

1. The letter should be concise and clear.

2. Grammatical mistakes should be avoided.

3. The letter must address the exact person.

4. All the information about the event should be relevant and clear.

5. The letter should be in simple style and tone.

6. The letter should have no place for misunderstandings.

7. The letter should be typed and not hand written.

Unit 14

Attract and Retain Customers

Attracting and retaining customers can be simple and difficult — simple because it is easy to create an impression, and difficult because the task involves marketing. A business has to provide products that will satisfy all kinds of customers — kids, teens, women, men, and so on. If a product cannot satisfy the customer, it will not create a demand, and ultimately result in a failure. A customer will not buy a product a second time unless it fulfills his needs the first time. A lesser known truth about product selling is that you should avoid "selling" and start "introducing" the product. The key to attracting and retaining customers is effective marketing.

There are many ways to attract and retain customers and it requires hard work, local knowledge, and reaching out to all customers. Good products and good services drive success.

Here are a few tips that will help you attract and retain customers:

Customer motivation, knowing the customer, first impression, brand confidence, patience, feedback adherence, elimination of doubts, quality, credibility, and innovation.

Unit 15

Modes of Transportation in Logistics

There are many modes of transportation, and each has its advantages and drawbacks. Goods can be transported by train, truck, plane, ship, or pipeline. The method used depends on time and cost.

Trains are usually used to transport bulk products that are low in value and must travel great distances.

Trucks can stop within a city and deliver goods direct to the market. A truck can start as soon as it is loaded. It is mostly used to transport high-value goods which travel short distances.

Air freight is quick although it is expensive. When speed is taken into consideration, this method will be more effective. Food and some urgently needed goods are usually delivered by air freight.

Ships have long been used for transportation. They are still the most important means of transportation in international trade now.

Commodities such as coal, grain, chemicals, and iron ore are often shipped by this means. Although it is a little slower, it is much less expensive. So far, most of our export goods have been transported by ship.

Pipelines are a special form of transportation. This form is being used for transporting gasoline, crude oil, and natural gas. Even some solids can be moved by pipelines.

With the expansion of international trade, the container service has become popular. The use of containers provides a highly efficient form of transport by road, rail, and air, which has been regarded as a mode of more efficient shipment.

Unit 16

What is Risk Management?

Risk management is the act of identifying and solving potential risks. A risk is defined as anything that has the potential to negatively affect a business or organization. Risk management is used by organizations and businesses to assess problems that either have occurred or will occur. After the risks, the business or organization then takes steps to reduce the risk or eliminate it completely.

Risk management serves as a way to protect a business's or organization's public face. The public opinion of an organization or business can drive its reputation up or down, which in turn can affect cash flow, potential investors, and present problems when trying to sell its services or goods. For example, if an exhibition company begins to expand faster than expected, one risk in particular that could arise is the lack of well-qualified employees. Bad employees, from employees that show up late to those who are rude to customers, can then reflect badly on the company's reputation for customer service. Identifying that potential risk and taking a step to fix it by implementing a company-wide policy for hiring employees is an example of risk management.